Golf at Yale

Michael Marsland

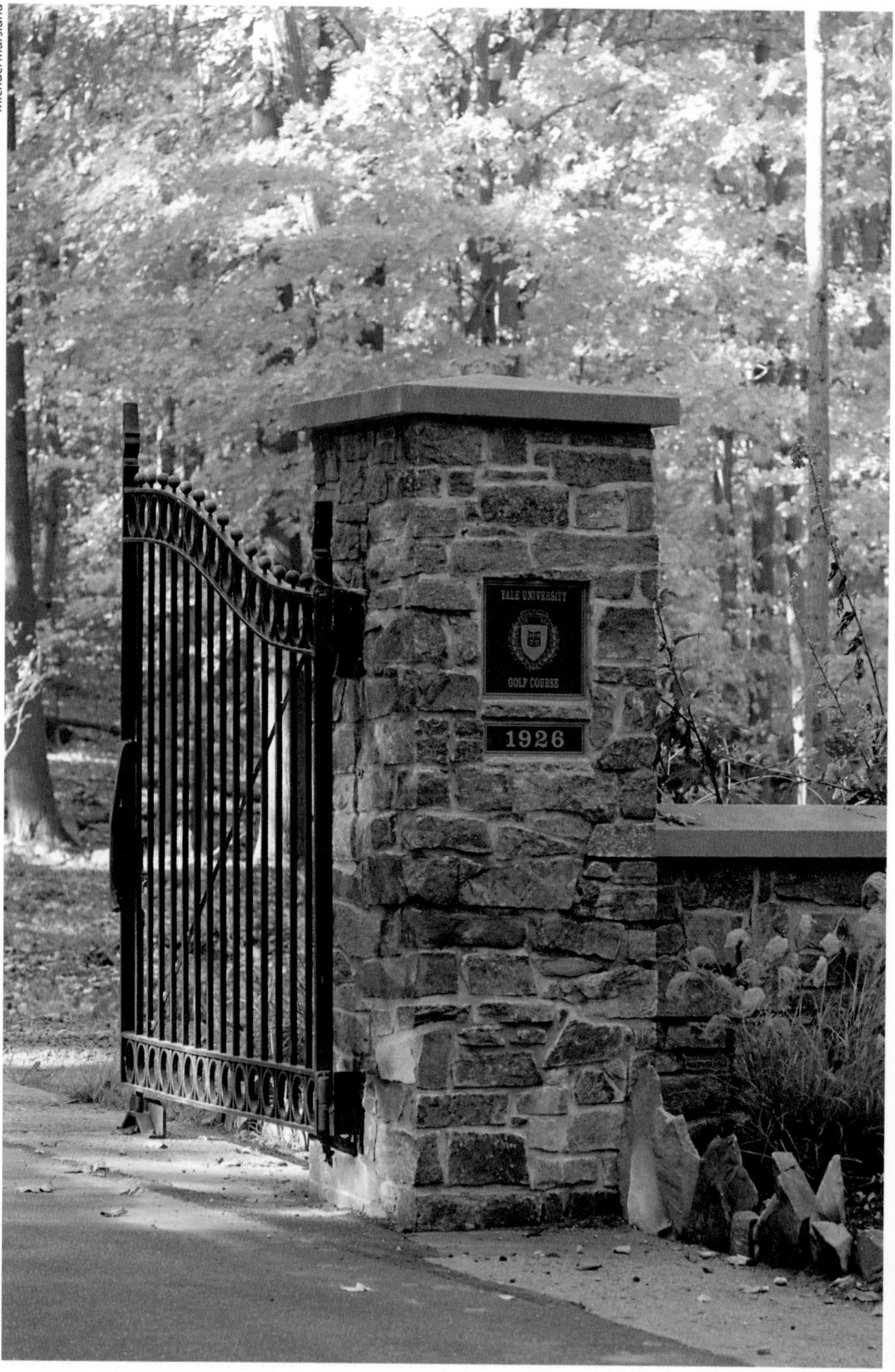

Golf at Yale

The Players, The Teams, The Course

John A. Godley and William W. Kelly

Marvelwood Press, New Haven, Connecticut

Marvelwood Press
New Haven, Connecticut

International Standard Book Number: 978-0-578-01510-1

Distributed by:
Department of Athletics
Yale University
P.O. Box 208216
New Haven, Connecticut 06520-8216
U.S.A.
Attn: Geoff Zonder, 203-432-4859
geoff.zonder@yale.edu

Printed by Phoenix Press, New Haven, Connecticut, U.S.A.
Layout and typography by MetaGlyfix, Bristol, Vermont, U.S.A.

Printed in U.S.A.

Contents

Frederic A. Borsodi | Varsity golfer and wartime test pilot

Edward L. Meister | 1940 team captain and longtime amateur

Arthur C. "Ace" Williams | 1943 team captain

Herbert Warren Wind | Golf writer, editor, and publisher

William H. "Widdy" Neale, Jr. | Athletics Department administrator and coach

Harry Meusel | Yale Golf Course superintendent

Joe Sullivan | Assistant pro, head pro, and golf team coach

Al Wilson | Golf team coach and head pro

William A. "Billy" Booe | 1948 team captain and PGA pro

Roy "Andy" Dye | Varsity golfer and course designer

Lincoln Roden III | 1952 team captain

Gerald F. "Jerry" Fehr | 1955 team captain

Edwin C. "Ned" Vare | 1956 team captain

David M. Ragaini | "Believe It or Not"

James Gamble Rogers III | 1968 team captain, clubhouse architect, and Yale Golf Association president

Theodore "Ted" Weiss | 1960 team captain

Robert "Bobby" Trent Jones, Jr. | Varsity golfer and course designer

Rees Jones | Golf course architect and "The Open Doctor II"

Roger G. Rulewich | Golf course architect

Herbert V. Kohler, Jr. | Innovative golf resort developer

Charles E. Fraser | Course developer and conservationist

Mark McCormack | Pioneer sports agent

Philip F. Nelson | Player, professor, and Golf Committee chairman

David Paterson | Director of Golf and men's and women's team coach

William Sperry Beinecke | Benefactor of the Yale Golf Course

William T. Lee | Eleven-time Yale Golf Club champion

Directional flag located behind the green, for blind second shot on the twelfth hole. Similar flags are at the third and eighth holes.

Preface

by John A. Godley
For fifty years, playing golf with family, friends, and strangers on the Yale golf course has enriched my life. My father introduced me to the joyful frustrations of the game and arranged for three lessons from the professional at a Donald Ross-designed course in Cincinnati. He told me golf stories about his encounters with Ben Hogan, Sam Snead, Patty Berg, and Arnold Palmer. My own first golf story involved an encounter with the then sixteen-year-old Jack Nicklaus at the Kenwood Country Club in Cincinnati, the site of the 1954 Western Open and occurred one week after he won the Ohio Open Championship.

I still clearly remember my very first drive on the first hole at the Yale Golf Course in 1958—I sliced it into Greist Pond! But my first drive on the eighteenth went long and straight to the base of the second hill, although my second shot then found the bunker at the top of that hill (thankfully the bunker is now gone!). There have been many more shots and rounds to remember: holes-in-one at the fifth and ninth, 73 strokes for eighteen holes, and 36 strokes on the front nine. But the most meaningful memories are of the people with whom I played. I was with Justin Shanley's father and with Hugh Dwyer for my holes-in-one and with Widdy Neale when I had my best front-nine score. With George Crowley and Ken Mackenzie I witnessed Carm Cozza's hole- in-one on the ninth. I cherish all the rounds with our sons, John and Mark, as they were growing up. One time, after our threesome went through Hugh Dwyer's group on the fifth hole, he asked me, "John, do you know what a rich man you are?" I didn't then, but I do now. On several occasions, my father joined us. On one beautiful spring day with the dogwoods in bloom on the sixteenth, he admitted, "This course is as beautiful and as good a test as Augusta National."

Over the years I heard many more stories, but unfortunately many of the storytellers were passing on, including Hugh Dwyer, Sam Spinner, Burt Resnik, Dick Tettlebach and many others. I didn't want that rich material to be lost. During a round of golf four years ago, Tom Beckett heard me telling some of those stories and suggested that I write a book. I was able to enlist my frequent golf partner, Bill Kelly, in that project. We collected more than 800 images and 300 documents and have conducted more than forty interviews. Tom provided me access to the University library and its links to other sources. He gave financial support to our student research assistants and for the publication of this book. With the luxury of time in retirement, I was able to do most of the research and some of the writing. But, the person who was essential for the successful completion of the on-line archive, the website, and this book was Bill Kelly. I suspect he would rather say that it took a good team and many supporters to write the story of one hundred twelve years of Yale golf.

by William W. Kelly

The pleasures and challenges of golf are among the most distinctive in the realm of sports. They are the source of my abiding affection for the Yale course and the motivations for my joining John in this project to explore the history of the course and all those who have played it over the decades.

Golf is special among modern sports because its venue, the golf course, is intended to be distinctive. Tennis courts, basketball courts, football fields, hockey rinks—almost every sport strains towards the standard and the uniform. Forest Hills is obviously a long way from the local town tennis courts, but tennis is a game of fixed dimensions and replicating conditions. Golf has always been the opposite. Every golf course is different, deliberately so. Every hole on every course is different. Every day of golf is different—morning conditions, evening conditions, the daily weather, the seasonal round, and the longer rhythms as a course changes over the years. All golfers know how profoundly this affects the experiences of playing.

And among golf courses, the Yale course is one of the most distinctively challenging. The genius of Charles B. Macdonald's design philosophy that Seth Raynor so masterfully implemented here at Yale was to learn deeply from some of the greatest holes in the Old World—such as the "Road" hole, "Biarritz," "Cape," and others—and to creatively transpose these designs to the diverse local landscapes of the New World. In New Haven their canvas was an immense and varied nature preserve of hilly woodlands, rocky outcrops, wet marshland, and ponds and streams. They shaped this into a contoured and corrugated masterpiece of complex shot options, of angles and elevations, of threatening tree lines and watery hazards, all made disarmingly attractive by the beautiful forested setting. At Yale, even if you can find the fairway with your drive on every hole in a round, you might still never have a flat lie and an even stance. It is forever challenging, forever frustrating, and forever rewarding.

Golf is distinctive among sports in a second way that speaks to the brilliance of its early practitioners, who realized that a game always played in such unique conditions needed a way to enable fair competition across players and courses. Thus was born the handicap system, which has had profound consequences for creating a sport that is not only enjoyable throughout life but is the only sport that can be played in fair and friendly competition with opponents of all levels. As a mediocre middle-handicapper myself, one day I can play a match against a scratch golfer like Yale's Bill Lee, now in the Connecticut Golf Hall of Fame, and then play an equally exciting match the next day with my daughter, who is just establishing a handicap in the 30s.

It is this quality of the sport that has brought me together in recent years with three men whose fellowship in golf has been a source of pleasure and an inspiration for this project. John Godley (Yale MD '62), George Crowley (Yale College '48), Ken McKenzie (Yale College '56), and I have played and competed together for years, and our early morning matches—four-ball, total score, throw the balls to pick pairs each game, no money, just pride and pleasure—have brought us the essence of the sporting experience. To these golfing companions I offer my sincere gratitude (though no Mulligans). And just as happily, I acknowledge my wife, Louisa Cunningham. For years she tolerated with bemusement my love of the game and this course. Now she too has taken up the game seriously, and we walk and play together many evenings, enjoying the course in the day's fading light.

Campus Golf

The fact that the links of the New Haven Golf Club are over a mile distance from the Campus partly accounts for the origin of a new phase of the game among the students. The Seniors, who have always reserved the privilege of playing games on the Campus ground, have instituted what is commonly known as 'Campus Golf.' This is played simply with a hockey stick and tennis ball, yet there is an opportunity for considerable dexterity in the play. A putter or driver is occasionally used, but the danger presented by the use of a real golf ball has prevented its adoption.

The newness of the game frequently furnishes amusement for spectators, though vexations to the players because the tennis balls which are to be seen rolling over the Campus in various directions are often picked up by a well-meaning passers-by and thrown back, much to the disgust of the player, who is endeavoring to approach a distant hole.

The regular course consists of six holes rudely cut in the ground and separated by almost equal distances. Although the position of the first 'tee' is not settled, the round is usually begun in the road just opposite the steps of Dwight Hall, the objective hole being just behind President Woolsey's statue. In this approach the Treasury Building must be circumvented, so that the hole is one of the most difficult in the course. The next drive is towards South Middle, and the hole lies a few feet away from the southwest corner towards the arch of at Vanderbilt. Turning back towards the west there is a short approach towards the third hole which is situated a few yards in front of the Chittenden Library. Then comes the longest drive of the course, but as the ground is perfectly level and there are no obstructions it is an easy matter to make the distance in four strokes. The hole is situated at that entrance of Lawrence which is next to Phelps Hall. The course extends then along the walk in front of Lawrence and Farnum to the fifth hole in the corner formed by Farnum and Battell Chapel. To complete the circuit the players returned to Dwight Hall, the sixth hole being near the steps leading towards Alumni Hall.

The best record so far made over this course, is twenty-three strokes, and is held by A.C. Sherwood '97. Almost every afternoon matches are played over this course, which excite considerable interest as to their outcome. The game seems to be growing daily in popularity and it would not be surprising if in a short time a regular tournament should be arranged amongst members of the Senior class. As there has been no objection on the part of the Faculty and with a careful observance of the rules relating to the Campus, there seems to be no reason why the game should not continue to flourish in the future.

*From the **Yale Alumni Weekly**, November 19, 1896, page 7*

1895–1926
Yale Golf's Early Years

Golf Comes to Yale
Robert D. Pryde and the first courses

As the *Yale Alumni Weekly* reported to its readers, the rage among seniors in the fall of 1896 was a new game, using hockey sticks and tennis balls to play golf through a makeshift course around campus buildings, which both fascinated and alarmed fellow students, faculty, and townspeople. For a more serious game, these same seniors shouldered a bag of clubs and climbed on the trolley car that took them out Prospect Street to the end of the line at Winchester Avenue, where they alighted to find a nine-hole course laid out across farmland just the year before. Golf had arrived at Yale with a passion.

John Reid, a transplanted Scotsman, played his first round of golf in America on February 22, 1888. The course was three holes that he had laid out in a pasture across from his home in Yonkers, New York. By November of that year, he had enlisted four friends to establish the St. Andrew's Golf Club with a longer course of six holes. They were known as the "Apple Tree Gang" because their clubhouse was a gnarly apple tree from which they hung their coats and their refreshments of scotch whiskey. They incorporated the St. Andrew's Golf Club in 1894, and, with The Country Club, the Chicago Golf Club, the Newport Golf Club, and Shinnecock Hills Golf Club, they founded the United States Golf Association (USGA) in 1895. The first USGA amateur champion was Charles Blair Macdonald of the Chicago Golf Club. John Reid and his "Apple

Tree Gang" kept moving their site until, in 1897, they built an eighteen-hole course that remains today at Hastings-on-Hudson, New York (the location has also been known as Mt. Hope and Ardsley).

Both John Reid and C. B. Macdonald were important figures in Yale golf, but to begin Yale's story we should go back three years earlier than Reid's fateful first round — to 1885 to the Scottish town of Tayport, in Fife, just north of the Old Course at St. Andrews. It was here that a 15-year-old Robert D. Pryde was learning to make and repair golf clubs as an apprentice in the shop of the Scotscraig Golf Club. The Scotscraig Golf Club was established in 1817 and is the thirteenth oldest club in the world. Pryde had attended Harris Academy in Dundee and the Technical College in Glasgow, where he qualified as a teacher in drawing. However, he was more drawn to golf and entered his apprenticeship. In 1892, at the age of twenty-two, he immigrated to America where, three years later, he found himself working as a cabinet-maker for David H. Clark in New Haven.

Robert D. Pryde in 1909

In the spring of 1895, Justus S. Hotchkiss, a retired New Haven businessman, decided that he wanted a cherry wood wardrobe built to match one in his home at the corner of Wall and Church Streets. He contacted David H. Clark, who sent his young employee, Robert Pryde, to begin the job. Golf was already in the mind of Justus Hotchkiss because he and Yale professor Theodore S. Woolsey had recently been given the task by the New Haven Lawn Club of exploring ways to start the new game of golf in New Haven. Hotchkiss discovered that the tradesman who was working in his home was from Scotland and was further delighted to learn of his love and knowledge of the game. Within a day of the meeting, Hotchkiss and Woolsey took Pryde around the city and together they found what Pryde later described as "suitable ground for a nine-hole course between Prospect Street and Winchester Avenue from Division to Goodrich Streets." Hotchkiss and Woolsey rented the land, and by the time that he had finished the cherry cabinet, Pryde had also laid out and built the course! It was open for play when the College convened in the fall of 1895.

The New Haven Golf Club was organized in 1895. At the beginning, the membership was mostly Yale professors and undergraduates. The undergraduates, according to Pryde, "took to golf as easily as a duck to water." They organized a separate Yale Golf Club in 1896, which was also known as the University Golf Club or The Golf Club. A team was chosen from among club members to play an inter-club match in

Yale Athletics Archives

The 1897 team, winners of the first intercollegiate championship

October against Brooklawn Country Club members. The team's first intercollegiate competition was in November against Columbia University.

At the New Haven Golf Club, Pryde was the greenskeeper. He made and repaired clubs and was "to instruct those who need it, and also to enter into a game with those who may be more advanced." From Scotland, he imported red coats for the Yale team, which they wore when they won the first intercollegiate championship, administered in 1897 by the USGA.

That first "national" tournament included teams from Yale, Harvard, Princeton, Columbia, and the University of Pennsylvania. Later, Dartmouth, Williams, and Cornell joined the competition. Yale, however, continued to dominate the intercollegiate championship, and, by 1913, it had captured

Members of the Yale Golf Club playing a stymie on the eighth green at the New Haven Golf Club, 1904

Yale Athletics Archives

twelve national titles. During this period, Pryde was at times referred to as "trainer" or as the "professional coach" of the golf team.

The New Haven Golf Club was expanded to eighteen holes, when it acquired the land from Goodrich Street to Millrock Road. Interestingly, it then covered 200 acres, which exceeds even the acreage of the current course. By 1898, professors and businessmen lobbied for another location where they could play without being crowded by undergraduates. The New Haven Country Club in Hamden was organized and, again, Pryde laid out the course. Twenty years later Willie Park, Jr., altered the course to its present configuration.

In 1913 University golfers faced a crisis when the rented land in New Haven began to be sold as large house lots. The first of those houses, built as a wedding present, is now the "Rosary" building of Albertus

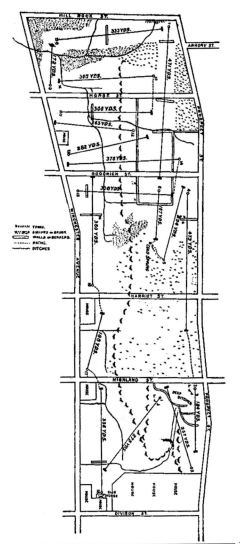

New Haven Museum

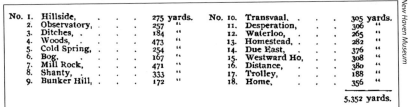

No.		yards.		No.		yards.
1.	Hillside,	275		10.	Transvaal,	305
2.	Observatory,	257		11.	Desperation,	306
3.	Ditches,	184		12.	Waterloo,	265
4.	Woods,	473		13.	Homestead,	282
5.	Cold Spring,	254		14.	Due East,	376
6.	Bog,	167		15.	Westward Ho,	308
7.	Mill Rock,	471		16.	Distance,	380
8.	Shanty,	333		17.	Trolley,	188
9.	Bunker Hill,	172		18.	Home,	356

5,352 yards.

The 18-hole layout with holes and yardages at the New Haven Golf Club, circa 1897

Race Brook Country Club, circa 1920

Magnus College. In response, the University and others purchased land in Orange and organized the Race Brook Country Club. Again, Pryde laid out the course and served as the club's Secretary-Treasurer from 1913 until 1937. One hundred and fifty memberships were set aside for Yale undergraduates, and Pryde continued as the unofficial golf team coach. However, even after it had been expanded to thirty-six holes, Race Brook was crowded. In a 1922 letter to the Yale Graduate Manager of Athletics, endorsing the proposal to build a Yale golf course, the team captain, Nathaniel Lovell, wrote that it was "due to the efforts of Mr. Pryde" that student memberships were maintained in spite of a waiting list for non-Yale members. Playing at Race Brook, Yale won three more intercollegiate championships. Indeed, the first fifteen of Yale's twenty-one national intercollegiate golf championships, a record that still stands, were led by Robert Pryde.

As secretary of the Connecticut Golf Association (CSGA), Robert Pryde wrote to the Yale Athletic Association on

December 20, 1928 to inform it that the Yale Golf Club had been elected to membership. He was active in USGA national committee work as well as in the CSGA. He retired in 1937 and spent the next year traveling around the world. Pryde visited golf courses in the western United States, Japan, South Africa, the Middle East, Europe, and the British Isles, about which he wrote periodic reports for the *New Haven Register* and the *Hartford Courant*.

In 1947 Pryde presented a paper before The New Haven Colony Historical Society on "The Early History of Golf in New Haven." On the occasion, he presented the Society with his collection of seventy-seven items of golf memorabilia. Among them were a red golf coat with a Yale University Golf Club monogram on the pocket (their retail cost in 1900 had been nine dollars) and an apple tree branch from what he said was the original Apple Tree Gang course, which he had probably obtained from the sons of John Reid. Regrettably, neither of these items remains at the Society today, although another branch of the famous apple tree is in the John Reid Room at

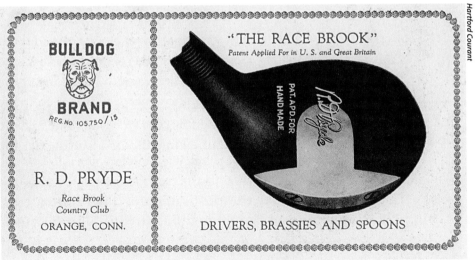

Advertisement for Robert D. Pryde's golf clubs, circa 1924

GOLF CLUBS

and

GOLF BAGS

In Large Assortment

We always have a fine stock of golf goods on hand. We
keep the best as well as the medium-priced goods and can
suit any desire.

GOLF BAGS

Plain Canvas Golf Bags, white or brown $1.00
Leather Trimmed Canvas Bags $2.50
Heavier Reinforced Leather Trimmed Bags $3.50
Rawhide Laced Leather Trimmed Bags $4.50
Regulation Traveling Bags with hood, strap and lock $7.50
Combination Bag with lock $8.00

ROBERT D. PRYDE'S GOLF CLUBS
IN FINE ASSORTMENT

Every golfer knows what these clubs are and there is no
need of talking about them.
Other Golf Clubs at moderate prices.
Lawn Tennis Rackets of all grades and prices, $1.50 up.
Wright & Ditson's Golf Balls, 45c. each, 3 for $1.25.
Spalding's Golf Balls.

COME TO US IF YOU WANT
GOLF OR SPORTING GOODS

Page's HARDWARE STORE

419 MAIN STREET

Advertisement for Robert D. Pryde's golf clubs,
circa 1924

the clubhouse of the St. Andrew's Golf Club, Hastings-on-Hudson, New York.

What do remain at the Colonial Historical Society (now the New Haven Museum) are examples of some of the innovative golf clubs that Pryde designed and made over his lifetime. The most important of these is a club he had patented in 1922, "with a reversible type of brass weight with a tongue running towards where the ball was hit, on the top of the club. This would tend to keep the ball low when it was hit, and if the weight was put in the bottom of the club it would tend to raise the ball off the ground." Pryde's advertising was direct: "Every golfer knows what these clubs are, and there is no need of talking about them." It was very effective because 50,000 of these club heads had been sold by the time of his presentation! Of course this same concept can be seen today in glossy golf magazine ads or on television, ballyhooed as the latest clubhead technology. These clubs bear the logos of Callaway or TaylorMade, not the Pryde bulldog logo.

Robert D. Pryde died in 1951 at his home on Racebrook Road, across from the third green of the country club. Certainly no one had more influence on Yale's early golf history than he.

Officers

Huntington Wilson, '97,	*President.*
Craig Colgate, '97, S.,	*Vice-President.*
J. I. Lineaweaver, '97,	*Secretary.*
W. B. Smith, '99,	*Treasurer.*
Roderick Terry, Jr., '98,	*Captain.*
W. R. Betts, '98,	*Vice-Captain.*

Executive Committee

Huntington Wilson, '97, A. R. E. Pinchot, '97, W. R. Betts, '98, John Reid, Jr., '99, F. C. Havemeyer, 1900.

Members

SENIORS.

T. M. Brown,	C. M. Fincke,	J. I. Lineaweaver,	A. R. E. Pinchot,	Philip Van Ingen,
Craig Colgate,	S. K. Gerard,	W. G. Low,	P. F. Ripley.	Karl Webb,
William Darrach,	C. E. Heffelfinger,	W. E. F. Moore,	A. C. Sherwood,	W. S. K. Wetmore,
H. L. De Forrest,	R. S. Hincks,	C. F. Mosle,	B. F. C. Thompson,	F. M. Wilson,
A. J. Draper,	H. T. Kneeland, Jr.,	H. C. Parke,	R. de P. Tytus,	H. Wilson.
R. F. Ely,	B. W. Kountze,	Stewart Patterson,		

Announcement of Yale student golf club, **Yale Alumni Weekly,** *1896*

John Reid, Jr., and Archibald M. Reid
Like father, like sons

John Reid, leader of the Apple Tree Gang, did not go to Yale, but he sent his two sons to New Haven. The older, John Reid, Jr., (Class of 1899) helped found the Yale University Golf Club in 1896 and was a member of the team that won the first intercollegiate championship, sponsored by the USGA in 1897. The same year, he won the University Championship and was elected vice-captain of the team. He was the individual intercollegiate champion in spring of 1898 and led the Yale squad to the intercollegiate championship in the fall. A year after he graduated, his brother Archibald (Class of 1904) arrived to continue the family golfing tradition. Archie was a member of the 1902 intercollegiate champion team and captain in 1904.

John Sr. was proud of his sons, but it seems he set a high standard. Both John Jr. and Archie competed successfully after college. One year, Archie was defeated in his United States Amateur match. His father, reading this in his morning newspaper at breakfast, was said to have turned gruffly to his wife, "I see where *your* son has lost a golf match!" But, it surely was *his* son John Jr., who, as the USGA secretary, presented the trophy to Francis Ouimet,

John Reid, Jr., Yale's first individual intercollegiate champion, 1898

Yale Athletics Archives

the winner of the US Open in 1913 at The Country Club in Brookline. Ouimet, an unheralded twenty-year old American amateur, bested the English professionals, Harry Vardon and Ted Ray, in a thirty-six hole playoff. Ouimet made "the shots heard round the world" in the "greatest game ever played," described so dramatically in Mark Frost's book of that title.

John Ellis Knowles
"Golf is for a lifetime"

We all hope to play golf for life, but few continue to play at the level of Ellis Knowles (Class of 1907). Born in Pensacola, Florida, he attended St. Paul's School in Garden City, Long Island. It was there as a fourteen-year-old that his interest in golf began, hitting balls against the wall of the school. Students were allowed to practice at the nearby Garden City Golf Club on weekdays. At age eighty, he told the *New York Times* that he still remembered the thrill of a member asking him one day, "Laddie, would you like to play a round with me?" That member was Walter J. Travis, who went on to win one British Amateur and two US Amateur titles.

As a sophomore at Yale, Knowles was runner-up to senior Robert Abbot for the intercollegiate golf championship in 1905. He won the championship as a senior in 1907. He settled in Rye, New York and became a partner in the Marine Transport Lines of New York City. He was prominent in the shipping industry and pioneered the development of chemical and LPG gas tanker design and operation.

One suspects that Ellis Knowles was prouder of his golfing record than his professional accomplishments. He won twenty-nine club championships: eight at Pensacola, one at Pine Valley, four at Round Hill in Greenwich, Connecticut, and sixteen at the Apawamis Golf Club in Rye. In 1936, at age fifty, he was listed as a thrteen-handicap by the Metropolitan Golf

Association, along with Jess Sweetser, age thirty-three. He was a member of the team of amateurs captained by Sweetser that played a charity exhibition against the US professional Ryder Cup team in 1933.

Ellis Knowles got better with age. The USGA Senior Amateur tournament was started in 1955. It was an expansion of a tournament conducted by the US Senior Golf Association, which itself had grown from a senior amateur event at the Apawamis Golf Club in the early 1900s. Knowles won the senior amateur tournament six times, and he captained the US senior amateur team that played teams from Canada and Britain at Pine Valley in 1959.

On his eightieth birthday, the members of Apawamis held a celebration for him, and the club pro (Jack Patroni), who himself had won the Met Open at age 56, toasted Mr. Knowles as one of the outstanding men in golf: "He has been scoring under 70 for the last forty years." Indeed, from age seventy-two on, Knowles felt he was off his game if he didn't shoot his age. (Knowles thought that his best round had been a 39-28 = 67 at Apawamis, way back in 1933.)

Robert A. Gardner
1912 team captain and elite athlete

Except for schooling and military service, Robert Gardner (Class of 1912) spent his entire life in the Chicago area, first in Hinsdale and later in Lake Forest. He was educated at Phillips Academy and then at Yale. He was a winner. As a senior at Phillips in 1908, he abandoned golf so that he could concentrate on pole vaulting and contribute to the victory over archrival Phillips Exeter Academy. The following year, as captain of the Yale freshman track team, he won the national intercollegiate pole vault championship and the USGA Amateur Championship, played that year at the C. B.

Macdonald-designed Chicago Golf Club. To get to the final, he defeated Walter J. Travis, the former British and US amateur champion. In the final, he defeated two-time champion, Chandler Egan. Because he was a freshman, Gardner couldn't play for the varsity golf team. Apparently the team didn't need him because it won the intercollegiate championship a week after Gardner's victory in the Amateur.

Gardner had stellar accomplishments in two sports throughout his Yale career. From 1910 through 1912, he was a member of the golf teams that extended Yale's streak of national intercollegiate championships to eight in a row, captaining the team in his senior year. He was also captain of the track team and set a world record of 13 feet 1 inch in winning the intercollegiate pole vault championship at Franklin Field in Philadelphia on June 2, 1912. Alas, the record was broken one week later by Marc Wright, a Dartmouth student, at the Olympic Trials at Harvard Stadium, where Gardner was not competing.

Gardner returned to Chicago to join the management of a local coal company and confined his golf to major competitions. In 1915, he entered the Amateur Championship along with other Yale graduates John Reid, Jr., and Max Behr. The favorites were "Chick" Evans, "Jerry" Travers, and Francis Ouimet, but

Yale Athletics Archives

Robert Gardner, circa 1915

Gardner won the tournament resoundingly. In September 1915, *Golf Illustrated* marveled that "his drives of 250-280 yards made Gardner appear like a Brobdingnagion golfer among Lilliputians," with "muscles of steel and nerves of iron."

The following year, the newly-married Gardner defended his amateur championship at Merion. Playing with an infected right index finger he advanced to the final but lost to "Chick" Evans. Gardner had earlier defeated a fourteen-year-old boy named Bobby Jones from Atlanta, who was playing in his first national championship. This match attracted 8,000 spectators, and Jones would remember that defeat as one of the most important events of his unparalleled career.

In 1917 Gardner teamed up with "Chick" Evans to play Bobby Jones and his friend Perry Adair in a match to raise money for the war effort. They attracted the largest crowd ever to see a match in Chicago (2,500) and raised one-thousand dollars. A month later, 16,000 spectators turned out to see Gardner and Evans and their female partners play a match. Then Gardner enlisted and spent World War I in France as a lieutenant in the field artillery. Returning from the war, he joined the brokerage firm of Mitchell, Hutchins & Company of New York and Chicago. He remained with the firm for the rest of his life and was a general partner when he died thirty-seven years later in 1956.

Golf remained Gardner's passion, and he remained one of America's leading amateurs of his era. He reached the final of the British Amateur in 1920, the best showing an American had made in sixteen years, and reached the finals of the US Amateur in 1921, losing the title to Jesse Guilford. He was a member of the first US Walker Cup team in 1922 and served as the playing captain in 1923, 1924, and 1926. (After 1924 it became a biennial event.) Here, too, Gardner was a winner — the team of Great Britain and Ireland didn't win until 1938! Late in life, he was a member of the 1949 US Senior golf team that defeated the British Senior team. And his sporting accomplishments were not limited to golf. In both 1916 and 1929, Gardner and Howard Linn won the national racquet pairs championship.

Nathaniel T. Lovell
1923 team captain

The Yale golf team won the national intercollegiate championship every year except one from 1905 to 1915 and then remained winless from 1916 to 1923. Jess Sweetser did win the individual championship in 1920, and Dexter Cummings won it in 1923. Yale's home course had changed from The New Haven Golf Club to Race Brook Country Club in 1913, and there were some who attributed Yale's long drought to this.

One of those was a Yale senior and the 1923 team captain, Nathaniel Lovell (Class of 1923), who wrote a letter on December 14, 1922 to J. T. Blossom, the Manager of Athletic Control, urging the construction of a new Yale golf course. "The present facilities are very inadequate," he charged, "and they may be denied to Yale men in the very near future." He continued, "The only club in New Haven that permits student members is the Race Brook Country Club. That this one club could not provide adequate facilities, was clearly demonstrated when we had our college tournament this fall, to help in the selection of the team in the spring. ... 67 entered, but since 20 did not belong to Race Brook, a third of the candidates were eliminated." He went on to suggest that if "there are 60 men at Yale who play well enough to try for the team, there are 400 men who would join a college course. (That is the estimated number of members needed to make a course self-supporting.)" He further pointed to the "increase in the popularity of golf" and the long waiting list for memberships at Race Brook, fifty of which were taken up by Yale students.

Finally Lovell speculated that if it were not for "the efforts of Mr. Pryde," the club secretary (and Yale coach), those student memberships would have already been eliminated. "We students cannot expect Mr. Pryde will be there forever."

Three years after his graduation, the university course had become a reality. But, like Seth Raynor, Nathaniel Lovell was not there to enjoy it. After graduation he had returned to his home in Manchester, New Hampshire. In 1925, he was the Manchester Country Club champion and held the amateur course record of 72. In January 1926, he sustained a minor scratch on his face, which became infected. A week later, Lovell was dead of what was identified as blood poisoning. It is interesting that less than two decades later, in 1942, the antibiotic that would likely have prevented his death was used for the first time on a patient with blood poisoning. This was penicillin, and it was administered by a Yale medical intern at New Haven Hospital, Rocco Fasinella, later a member of the Yale Golf Club.

Chester B. Bowles
1924 team captain, governor, and diplomat

Chester Bowles (Class of 1924) was born in Springfield, Massachusetts and attended Choate before going to Yale. In 1924, as a senior, he was captain of the golf team that won the intercollegiate championship, although he was not one of the four players whose scores counted toward the win. In the opening match of that season, he had been paired with his teammate, Dexter Cummings, the 1923 individual intercollegiate champion, and they lost to a team from the Westchester Biltmore Country Club in Rye, New York. In 1923 Bowles had lost his match in the Apawamis Invitational. He did not play in the intercollegiate team competition at the end of the season, but he did compete in the individual championship, losing in the second round. Why was he elected team captain? It may well be that the qualities that made Bowles successful in advertising, politics, and diplomacy were evident even then to his constituents.

Bowles wrote later that "as a college senior, in 1924, I determined to spend my life in government," observing that he was one of a few in class for whom a public career held any interest. First he went to New York and got a job as a $25 per week copywriter in an advertising agency. During the Great Depression of 1929 he started his own advertising firm with another Yale graduate, William Benton. It was highly successful, but Bowles was not satisfied by monetary rewards alone. The events of December 7, 1941 provided him the opportunity he had been seeking.

Because of an ear problem Bowles was rejected when he tried to enlist in the Navy. He accepted a position as director of the Office of Price Administration in Connecticut. In 1943, President Roosevelt appointed him general manager of the Federal Price Administration. He was the Director of Economic Stability, when he ran unsuccessfully for governor of Connecticut in 1946. He became governor in 1948. He was named US Ambassador to India in 1951 and

Chester Bowles in a 1924 golf team photo

again in 1961. Between those posts he served in the House of Representatives from Connecticut's second district. Bowles wrote seven books setting forth his philosophy of domestic and foreign policy.

Jesse W. "Jess" Sweetser
Winner of the Amateur Slam

The 1920s in America was the decade when sport stars became superheroes and celebrities to an expanding mass public culture. Babe Ruth in baseball, William T. "Bill" Tilden in tennis, Jack Dempsey and Gene Tunney in the ring, and Bobby Jones on the links put spectator sports at the center of American public attention. Bobby Jones is one of the preeminent figures in golf history, and his dominance of the game during the 1920s electrified the nation and propelled the popularity of golf. His feat of winning the "Grand Slam" of all four major championships of the era in a single year (the 1930 US and British Amateur Championships and the 1930 US and British Opens) has still never been matched.

Against this, all other golfers of his time came up short, but several, including Jess Sweetser (Class of 1923 S), earned broad acclaim and enduring accomplishments of their own. Indeed, what Jess Sweetser accomplished in his amateur golf career is unmatched even by Jones, his friend and fellow amateur competitor. In winning all three of the major amateur championships, Sweetser achieved his own slam, the "Amateur Slam" we might say, a trio of victories that no one, including Jones, Jack Nicklaus, or Tiger Woods, has done.

Jess Sweetser was born in St. Louis, Missouri and attended Exeter Academy before entering Yale in 1920. At both schools he participated in what was considered a "major" sport, track, and a "minor" sport, golf, but it was in the latter that he truly excelled. As a Yale freshman in 1920, Sweetser took the National Intercollegiate Championship at the Greenwich Country Club and was runner-up the following year. He played in the US Open in 1921, finishing in eleventh place while still a teenager. He followed that by winning the Metropolitan Championship in 1922, while a junior at Yale.

Even greater accomplishments were soon in store for Sweetser, who faced a formidable line-up of opponents at the US Amateur later in 1922 at The Country Club in Brookline. The event attracted more than sixty reporters, and Sweetser proved to be the talk of golf that year, the "leading giant killer," as he successively defeated Willie Hunter (the British Amateur champion), then Jesse Guilford (the reigning US Amateur champion), before facing Bobby Jones, already known as the best amateur golfer in the world. Sweetser won easily against Jones, 8-and-7, in a thirty-six-hole match during which he set a new course record with a score of 69. He then completed his sweep by defeating Charles "Chick" Evans, Jr., (winner of the 1916 US Open and US Amateur and the 1920 US Amateur) to take the crown. The press was in awe. J. Lewis Brown, then editor of *Golf Illustrated,* wrote in the October issue that year, "Although comparisons are odious, I could not but reflect on the same National Championship at Brookline in 1913 (when Francis Ouimet defeated Vardon and Ray). Each of these was alike, in that they produced two new American boys as national heroes, and this is all the more striking, because of the fact that The Country Club was the setting for both of these great events."

Jess W. Sweetser, New York, National Amateur Champion

In his senior year and for several years after his graduation in 1923, Sweetser served on the Yale Golf Committee. He was present when the Committee toured the Greist estate on a bitter cold day in February of 1923 to determine if the Tompkins' gift would be an appropriate site for a golf course.

Records indicate that he could subsequently attend only a few meetings of the golf committee because of his numerous golf commitments; pairings with his friend Bobby Jones were especially popular. When he and Jones (then a Harvard Law School student) played against Gene Sarazen and Walter Hagen at Winged Foot in Mamaroneck, New York, on October 28, 1923, the *New York Times* reported the next day that "3,000 excited spectators rushed from hole to hole" to see the students beat the professionals 1 up.

American Golfer, September 23, 1922

Jess W. Sweetser as the new 1922 US Amateur Champion

Some of Sweetser's greatest exploits came as a member of the first five US teams in the Walker Cup Match, initiated in 1920 between the USGA and the Royal & Ancient Golf Club of St. Andrews. As a Yale junior, Sweetser played in the first official match in 1922 at National Golf Links of America and then traveled with Jones and others in the spring of 1923 to play the Great Britain and Ireland team at the Old Course. The United States, captained by Robert Gardner, won 6 1/2 to 5 1/2. Thereafter, the Cup

Augusta National Historic Imagery

*(from left) Bobby Jones, Jess Sweetser, Gene Sarazen, and Walter Hagen at Winged Foot
Golf Club, October 28, 1923*

Match was played every other year, with Sweetser named to the team in 1924, 1926, 1928, and 1932.

Yale was not entirely accommodating to Sweetser, especially in his final year in 1923. Although he was then the reigning US Amateur champion, it took a special meeting of the scholarship committee of the Yale Sheffield Scientific School to get him on the boat for Scotland. Reluctantly, the faculty allowed "absence from his classroom recitations, but he must make up the work before the end of the term." Furthermore, the committee ruled that he would not be allowed to play with the varsity golf team that spring. This apparently irritated the Athletic Board of Control, which immediately passed a resolution on April 9 that "any undergraduate who wins a national title in tennis or golf (minor sports) would receive automatically a major 'Y'" (as reported in the *New York Times* the next day). The importance of this "Y" to Sweetser is clearly seen in the US team photograph taken at the 1923 Walker Cup matches, where he sits in the center, proudly wearing his Yale Y sweater over his jacket and tie!

Even more than his US Amateur title, perhaps Sweetser's most dramatic individual victory came in 1926, when he was the first American-born man ever to win the British Amateur. Nothing is more boring than a shot-by-shot description of a golf match, unless it is done by Herbert Warren Wind, Yale Class of 1937, and the dean of American golf writers. The following is his account of Sweetser's exploits from his book *The Story of American Golf* (on pp. 189-92 in the 1975 Third Edition).

> *The odd thing was that Jess, the strong boy, won his British Amateur crown when his body was wracked with flu, and incipient tuberculosis. No man has ever won a major athletic contest in poorer health. It was quite a saga of courage.*

Jess had married in February of '26. Happiness and regular meals at home plus a modicum of golf had put some extra pounds on him. He planned to work them off by exercising in the gym aboard the ship that was carrying the Walker Cup team to Britain. Sweating pleasantly after one workout, Jess decided to take a dip in the pool ... and his miseries began. His sinuses began to kick up, and he spent the rest of the passage stretched out on a deck chair, hoping that he would snap back once he was on land again. He didn't. In the raw air of early spring in England and Scotland, his cold was aggravated into an enervating flu. At Muirfield,

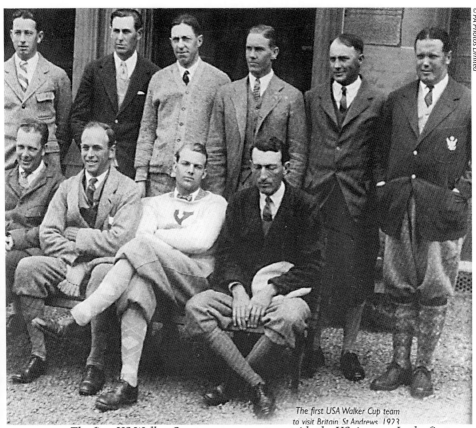

The first USA Walker Cup team to visit Britain St Andrews 1923

The first US Walker Cup team to compete outside the US, in 1923. In the first row, Jess W. Sweetser is wearing his major Y sweater.

where the American team was entered in the British Amateur previous to the Cup Match at St. Andrews, Jess got in only two practice rounds and stayed in his room the remainder of the time trying to nurse himself back into shape. He felt so rotten on the morning he was scheduled for his first-round match that, much as he wanted to play in the championship, he felt that there was no other course than to default. He stayed in the tournament only because his opponent chose to default before Jess did. After lunch — there were times during the tournament when Jess could hold hardly more than orange juice — he forced himself to go out and play his second-round match. He managed to win and staggered wearily into the clubhouse.

Day after day it was the same story. A masseur from Edinburgh, contacted by Henry Lapham of the American party, would work up Jess' circulation before he went out against his morning opponent. At lunch Jess would drink fruit juices and try a slice or two of beef, and push himself out to the tee for his afternoon match. He did no partying in the evening — took a hot bath and went straight to bed. His attitude was good. He wasn't expecting to win and he didn't worry when it took him six or seven holes to warm up. He kept hitting his shots, and eventually he caught and passed his opponents, although quite a few of Jess' matches went to the eighteenth hole. He defeated Ouimet on the eighteenth by pumping a beautiful second shot through the mist to the green. Against Robert Scott, he played another clinching approach on the home hole, toeing in his favorite 4-iron and punching it low and hard. Jess didn't have the energy at Muirfield to goad himself on with fight talks, but he hummed to himself as he went along, usually "Somebody Loves Me." He kept on winning.

In the semi-final round Jess came up against the Honorable W. G. Brownlow (later Lord Lurgan), a good golfer albeit a chap of weird sartorial tastes. Brownlow played in a small peaked cap, a long clerk's coat, and black silk gloves. Jess, for once, started fast and picked up two holes on Brownlow early in the match, but he could make no further headway against his opponent's neat if not spectacular golf. On the seventeenth, however, this two-hole margin became dormie for Jess, and the match looked as good as over when he laid his third twelve feet from the pin with Brownlow forty-five rolling feet away in the same number of strokes. The game Irish dandy had been putting, and putting well, with an orthodox blade putter. Now, as he eyed his long route to the cup, he switched to a wide-soled, wooden-headed Gassiat model and proceeded to hole his cross-country putt. Jess then missed his, but was still dormie one with the home hole coming up. Once again Jess played the eighteenth perfectly. He was nicely inside Brownlow on the green, eighteen feet away from his opponent's thirty-five. His half seemed certain. And then the incredible Brownlow took his Gassiat in his black silk gloves and sent his ball trickling over the subtle rolls of the home green and into the very center of the cup. Jess made a courageous try for his putt but slid it by the rim of the cup.

By this time, the match had taken on an unreal atmosphere. Jess exhausted by the sudden turn of events, Brownlow unnaturally serene, both of them performing as if they were caught in the webbing of a dream. On the first extra hole, Brownlow had a big opening when Jess found a trap on his second, but Brownlow misfired with his Gassiat, taking three from twenty-five feet after slipping fifteen feet by on his first. On the 20th Jess went ten feet past the cup on his approach putt but Brownlow, timorous after his error on the 19th, fell nine feet short on his. Jess knocked in his 10-footer, and Brownlow stepped up and coolly holed his 9-footer. On the 21st tee the young Irishman finally cracked. He

*looked up badly on his drive. Jess smashed his two hundred
and sixty yards down the fairway, and his faultless approach
closed out the dramatic duel between two dead-game golfers.*

*The final between Jess and Archie Simpson, an East
Coast Scotsman, was bound to be a letdown after the
Sweetser-Brownlow match. Simpson didn't play nearly as
well as he had against Andrew Jamieson in the semi-finals,
and Jess won 8 and 6 after a dull match in which the outcome
was never in doubt.*

It may have been a dull finals, but Wind curiously doesn't
relate the considerable drama at the outset. Sweetser was
indeed feeling sicker and sicker, but when he arrived at the
tee for his finals' match, his opponent, Simpson, was missing.
The rules required that Simpson forfeit, but Sweetser thought
it would be an unsporting resolution. Rather than seizing on
the opportunity, he took himself off to the clubhouse W. C.
and refused to come out until Simpson showed up. In fact, as
Steve Eubank recently described in *Sports Illustrated* (July 14,
2008), Simpson's car had broken down just out of town, and
he finally came toiling up to the tee on a borrowed bicycle with
his golf bag jangling over his shoulder. The match took place
because of the generous gesture and the quick thinking
Sweetser.

He had little time, though, to savor his success, and,
indeed, brought further suffering upon himself by insisting
on heading to the Walker Cup matches at St. Andrews. Wind
goes on to relate:

*Jess' condition became worse after he was driven to St.
Andrews on a very cold day. He asked to play and managed
to win both his singles and foursome in the Walker Cup
Match with a continuation of his impeccable golf, and then
suffered a severe chest hemorrhage. Jess pleaded with the
doctors to let him sail — he was frightened that he might not
come home alive — and the doctors at length gave in. They*

shot him full of heroin and gave O. B. Keeler instructions on how to inject the drug if Jess suffered a relapse on board ship. Jess did have one more hemorrhage, but the heroin kept him going …. He reached home so utterly shattered that only after a full year of convalescence at Asheville did he begin to look and feel like the Jess Sweetser of old.

While Sweetser was a member of the National Golf Links of America from 1935 to 1945, he finally met C. B. Macdonald, although he never had an opportunity to play with him. Sweetser later described Macdonald as a "great fellow and great character," although Sweetser confirmed in an interview late in his life that, to his knowledge, Macdonald never had an opportunity to visit the Yale Golf Course after its construction.

Sweetser's professional career was in business. He began as a stockbroker in New York and later joined the Martin Marietta Aircraft Corporation, from which he retired as a vice-president in 1967. But his passion was always golf. He remained an important figure in the USGA (serving as treasurer for much of the 1940s) and with the Walker Cup teams. In 1966, he captained the Eisenhower Trophy team and in 1967 and in 1973 served as captain of the USA Walker Cup team. In 1986 Sweetser was honored by the USGA with its Bob Jones Award, given annually since 1955 to recognize distinguished sportsmanship in golf.

Sweetser had treasured his time in Asheville and later visited often. He was a member at the highly regarded Biltmore Forest Country Club, which had opened in 1922, the year he first arrived in Ashville. Each Memorial Day weekend, the club holds a popular tournament in Sweetser's honor and retains some of his memorabilia and records.

Shortly before he died in 1989, David Paterson interviewed Sweetser who again expressed his lifelong admiration for Jones, insisting, "During the 1920s, my record in amateur play was as good or better than all others, except for Bob Jones." Paterson later asked where he wished his most prized trophies to be displayed. Sweetser had decided that his British Amateur trophy would go to Golf House, the USGA headquarters, and his Amateur trophy and Bob Jones award to Burning Tree. He was a member of the Burning Tree Club from 1950 until his death. He was a good friend of fellow member, Robert Trent Jones, and sponsored the membership of Ken Venturi, the first professional golfer to join the club. After Sweetser died, Robert Sommers memorialized him in the *USGA Golf Journal* of July 1989.

> *I only saw Jess Sweetser play once. It was 1957, and he was 55 years old, a vice president of the Glen L. Martin Company, a manufacturer of aircraft, out for a round with some friends at the Green Spring Valley Hunt Club, a pleasant although not particularly demanding course on the outskirts of Baltimore. I tagged along to watch. He shot 69 with little effort. A week or so earlier he had shot 64 at the Elkridge Club, another Baltimore course, and 66 at Burning Tree, near Washington. A burly man, standing a bit over six feet, with huge forearms and bushy eyebrows, he did not have a picture swing, but it was efficient. Jess had left competitive golf long before I met him, and he played only weekend mixed four-balls at his club and annual invitation events, but watching him that day left me certain he could have beaten anybody.*

Herbert Warren Wind once wrote that there are three kinds of golf—golf, tournament golf, and major championship golf. Through the decades, Yale golfers have won their share of tournaments and regular championships, but Sweetser's "Amateur Slam" of the National Intercollegiate Championship in 1920, the US Amateur Championship in 1922, and the British Amateur Championship in 1926 remains a unique accomplishment in golf history. It puts Sweetser at the pinnacle of Yale golf history.

Dexter Cummings
1925 team captain

When Dexter Cummings (Class of 1925) won
his second consecutive individual intercollegiate golf championship in 1924, the *New
York Times* identified him as "a member of
America's greatest golfing family." Dexter and
his sister Edith learned to play golf from their
parents at the Onwentsia Club in Lake Forest
Illinois, a venerable course laid out in 1895
and site of the 1906 US Open. Both his
mother and father had been club champions.

Cummings won his first individual intercollegiate championship in 1923 at Simonoy
Country Club in Bronxville, New York. He
defeated the Princeton captain and one of
the leading amateurs of that time, Rudy
Knepper. In 1924, at Greenwich Country
Club, the Yale team won the national championship, and Cummings was again the individual champion, beating W. H. Taft of
Dartmouth.

Sister Edith Cummings was getting even
more recognition at this time. She won both
the US and British Women's Amateur championships in 1923. In 1924 she played an
extensive schedule, coast to coast. In August
she teamed with Marion Hollis, the 1921
amateur champion, to defeat Glenna Collett
and her partner in an exhibition at the Seth
Raynor-designed Country Club of Fairfield.
Two days later she appeared on the cover of
Time magazine.

Yale Athletics Archives

*Dexter Cummings in a 1925 golf
team photo*

Dexter Cummings was captain of the 1925 team that again won the national championship, and he graduated Phi Beta Kappa. Back home in Lake Forest that summer, he was the medalist in the Western Amateur by seven strokes over his old rival, Rudy Knepper. He returned to Yale in June 1926, scheduled to play an exhibition match that would honor the new course, partnering with Jess Sweetser against Francis Ouimet and Jesse Guilford. Only Cummings was able to play that day, scoring a 76.

Except for service as a US Navel officer during World War II, Cummings remained in Lake Forest. He married, had three children, eleven grandchildren, and three great grand-children. He became chairman of the Adwell Corporation, a corporate farm in Illinois with more than fourteen thousand tillable acres. All this left no time for competitive golf, other than at the Onwentsia Club. Cummings's sister Edith, too, after winning the Western Amateur in 1924, moved on to other pursuits — big game in the Yukon, riding, painting, and traveling throughout Europe and Canada. In 1934 she married Curtis Munson, Yale Class of 1916.

Sidney W. Noyes, Jr.
Threepeat national championship team member

Before his death in 2003, Sidney Noyes (Class of 1933) recounted a memory that could have come from "The Legend of Bagger Vance," although Noyes had neither read the book nor seen the film. He had just finished the first qualifying round of the 1930 US Amateur Championship at Merion Cricket Club in Ardmore, Pennsylvania. His score of 70 left him just one shot behind the leader, Bobby Jones. While Noyes was changing his shoes in the locker room (just like the young Bagger Vance), Jones stopped to congratulate him on his fine play and wish him luck in the second round. Noyes followed his 70 with a 77, easily qualifying for the championship, but lost in the second round of match play. Jones shot 69-73 to lead the qualifiers and went on the win the match play title to complete the grand slam.

Noyes was born in Portland, Maine in 1910. His mother refused to allow him and his three brothers to play football, which was then the prestige school sport. They turned instead to golf, especially when the family moved into a mansion adjacent to the storied Ardsley Golf Club. Noyes started winning early in life. In 1924, at the age of fourteen, he won the second flight of the Maine Amateur Championship and, three years later, took the first flight of the Championship as well as the New York Metropolitan Golf Association Junior Championship and the Westchester County Junior Championship. He repeated both championships the next year, in 1928, and made his initial foray into the US Amateur Championship. As a student at the Hotchkiss School, Noyes won the Interscholastic Golf Association Championship before entering Yale in the fall of 1929. He earned three major Y letters by playing consistently in medal play qualifiers, taking second place in the 1931, 1932, and 1933 National Intercollegiate Championships. His performances helped Yale win all three team championships. His best match play was in reaching the 1932 semifinals before losing to J. W. Fisher of Michigan, the eventual winner.

Noyes finally qualified for match play in the 1932 US Amateur at Five Farms in Baltimore, only to lose to Francis Ouimet in the second round. He qualified again in 1933 at the Kenwood Country Club in Cincinnati, Ohio, shooting a four-under par 31 on the final nine. He advanced to the quarter-finals, losing to Max Marston on the thirty-eighth hole. It was during this match that Noyes was penalized with loss of hole for picking up a pear in front of his ball. Today that would be regarded as a loose impediment. Marston went on to the final.

In the 1934 US Amateur at The Country Club in Brookline, he reached the third round of match play, even though he was now working for Manufacturers Trust Co. in New York and had little time to practice. The same year, Bobby Jones invited him to his first invitational tournament, which was to become the Masters, but Noyes reluctantly declined, given the demands of his job.

The year 1935 was perhaps Noyes's best year. He qualified for the 1935 US Open Championship at Oakmont in Pittsburgh, noting proudly in his journal that at last he was able to play with the pros. He won the Green Meadow Country Club Invitational, which attracted many of the top amateurs, and again won the Maine Amateur Championship. He partic-

The 1932 Golf Team. Top, left to right: Hamilton Wright; Ben Thomson (coach); Dave Gamble; Dave Ramsey (manager); Burt Resnik. Bottom, left to right: Pierpont Warner, Sidney Noyes, Dan England (captain) John Parker, H. Law Weatherwax

Yale Athletics Archives

ipated in an exhibition match at the Ardsley Country Club, partnering with the club professional, Dave Whyte, against Sam Parks, the US Open Champion, and long-hitting Jimmy Thompson, the US Open runner-up.

Noyes married Clare Smith of Pine Orchard, Connecticut that same year, and golf gradually became secondary to family and work. In 1936, he qualified for one more US Amateur at the Garden City Golf Club on Long Island but lost in the first round of match-play. Like many golfers of the time, his career was interrupted by military service in World War II. His later competitive golf was limited to Connecticut state and local New Haven club events. Noyes donated his memorabilia to Yale, and his son George presented his father's trophies and medals, where they remain on display at the David Paterson Indoor Golf Technology Center in the Payne Whitney Gymnasium.

Max Behr
Yale's first graduate to design golf courses

The first Yale graduate to become a golf course architect was Max Howell Behr (Class of 1905). He was born in New York City and attended Lawrenceville School in New Jersey before entering Yale. Golf was in Behr's blood. His Scottish grandfather and father were founders of the St. Andrew's Golf Club in Yonkers, New York, in 1888. Before coming to Yale, he was a "scratch player" who was a medalist (though not a winner) of the President's Cup at the Morris (New Jersey) Country Club. His pattern of doing well without winning continued at Yale. The 1902 intercollegiate championship was held in the spring, and the Yale varsity won, but Max was on the freshman team. The tournament was moved to the fall, and Harvard won in 1902, 1903, and 1904. In 1903 Behr was the only Yale player to win a match against Harvard, and, in 1904, he tied the celebrated Harvard captain, H. Chandler Egan, over thirty-six holes. Yale won the 1905 fall championship, but Max had graduated in the spring.

Leaving Yale, Behr concentrated on playing the game seriously. Again he fell short, losing to Jerome Travers (who was later the 1915 US Open Champion) in the finals of the 1907 and 1908 New Jersey Amateur and the finals of the 1908 US Amateur. In 1909 he succeeded in winning the New Jersey Amateur Championship and successfully defended in 1910 against Travers. He again bested Travers and C. B. Macdonald as the medalist in the first tournament played at the National Golf Links of America in 1910. Behr played in the US Amateur and British Open Championship in 1929, using the "floater" ball.

From 1914 to 1918 Behr was the first editor of *Golf Illustrated* magazine. But the untimely death of his young wife prompted a change in his life, and, at the age of 34, Behr moved to California and took up course design. George Bahto, in his *Evangelist of Golf*, attributes Behr's early inspiration to his college coach, Robert Pryde, who not only taught him about the game but also "pointed out the subtle interplays of design and nature, and what worked and what did not when it came to course design and construction."

In the 1920s, the golf boom was sweeping Southern California, and Behr arrived with somewhat radical ideas. For instance, he didn't believe in adding rough to his courses, preferring "to use natural terrain and bunkers to defend (his) greens from every conceivable angle." Between 1922 and 1927, about a dozen of his courses were built in California. He started with the Hacienda Golf Club in 1922 and ended with Rancho Santa Fe Golf Club in 1927. He remodeled the Victoria Club in 1923, the Brentwood Country Club in 1925, and consulted on the remodeling of the Olympic Club's Lake Course in 1926.

Max Behr (left) and Dr. Alister Mackenzie at the Old Course, St. Andrews Scotland, 1924

Behr's two best known courses are Lakeside in Hollywood and Rancho Santa Fe near San Diego. Lakeside Golf Club was located just across the Los Angles River from Universal Studios. It was then, and still is, a favorite of the movie colony. Bing Crosby was the 1937 club champion.

Rancho Santa Fe Golf Club (RSFGC), which opened in 1929, was the last course that Behr designed. He was recommended for the job by Dr. Alistair Mackenzie, who had had to turn down the job because he was designing Cypress Point. (He finished the work of Seth Raynor, the original designer who died unexpectedly after completing a routing plan). Behr received a fee of $9,000 for RSFGC (whereas Mackenzie received only $8,000 for Cypress Point). Behr wrote at the time that "a new principle of golf course design has been put into effect at Rancho Santa Fe which permits the average golfer, even the beginner, to enjoy the round without constantly being in trouble and yet at the same time offers the expert a serious and exciting test of golf. Not a single hazard has been constructed with the idea of penalizing errors of skill. On the contrary, the hazards are located with the sole object of defending the hole." Rancho Santa Fe was the site of the first Pro-Am tournament (from 1937-42), the Bing Crosby "Clam-bake" that is now the National Pro-Am at Pebble Beach. The 1954 San Diego Open was held there, as was the 2006 USGA Junior Amateur. Golfing greats of every era, from Walter Hagen and Babe Zaharias to Annika Sorenstam and Tiger Woods, have played the course. Today it is the home course of Phil Mickelson.

The Great Depression put an end to Behr's design business, but he continued to write about course design and construction and the rules of golf and to advocate acceptance of a standard golf ball that floats in water. He was last heard from at the USGA annual meeting in Portland, during the Amateur Championship in 1937. There he presented a resolution to the

USGA advocating the "floater," contending that "the ball manufacturers ... dictate the sort of golf that is played, and ... that mere brawn off the tee receives an unfair reward." The resolution was not adopted, although similar sentiments have been advanced by Donald Ross in the same decade and Jack Nicklaus more recently.

Late in life Max Behr became outspoken in his political views, and he even devised a religion based on numbers. However, his lasting legacies remain the great golf courses he designed in southern California.

William B. Langford
National championship team member and golf
architect

Of all the Yale graduate golf course architects, William Langford (Class of 1910 S) had the longest and most productive career but remains the least well known. He was born in Austin, Illinois and learned to play golf as part of his rehabilitation from childhood polio. Bill Langford played on the golf teams that won the national championship every year he was at Yale. After graduation, he went to Columbia University to study mining engineering but remained above ground! In 1917 he began a fifty-year, golf course construction collaboration with Theodore Moreau. With Langford doing the designs and Moreau directing their eighty-person construction crew, the pair built more than 200 courses mostly in the Midwest, during the next half century.

Mark Chalfant has written a delightful essay about Langford's designs, subtitled "Making Waves in the Heartland." He describes a Langford course as fun to play, full of variety, strategically interesting with routing that is often bold and expansive. In 1919, Langford himself wrote, "Hazards should be placed so that any player can avoid them if he gauges his ability correctly, so that these obstacles will make every man's game more interesting, no matter what class player he is." His affection for the common man was also reflected in his proposal to build six-hole courses to accommodate the budget and the schedule of a busy working man. Even though this idea was not adopted, he did operate several daily-fee courses in Illinois. Chalfant summarizes Langford's design style:

> It seems rather clear that his tendencies and thematic concerns often bear striking similarities to the gifted disciples of Charles Blair Macdonald, Seth Raynor and Charles Banks. Large pushed up greens that are peppered with intense undulation and also defended by deep bunkers with steep walls are shared motifs. However, Langford rarely relied on template holes derived from acclaimed paradigms imported from the British Isles or France. Occasionally, he seemed to mildly allude to the Biarritz or Redan.

The course and place names of Bill Langford's best known designs evoke a different time and place, such as Wakonda in Des Moines, Iowa, Harrison Hills in Attica, Indiana, Skokie in Skokie, Illinois, Maxinkuckee in Culver, Indiana (played often by Roy and Pete and Alice Dye early in their careers), Ozaukee in Mequon, Wisconsin,

Yale Athletics Archives

Yale Varsity Golf Team of 1909 posing at the "Yale Fence." From left: William B. Langford, 1910S; Buckingham P. Merriman, 1910, manager; Drake Lightner, 1909; Charles E. VanVleck, 1909, captain; Kent S. Clow, 1910; Karl E. Mosser, 1911; Robert Y. Hayne,1909

Lawsonia in Green Lake, Wisconsin, and Happy Hollow in Omaha, Nebraska.

He seems like a fellow whom you would like to have in your foursome.

Samuel F. B. Morse
Developer and conservationist

There is an historical link between the Yale Golf Course, currently rated the number one university course in the country, and Pebble Beach Golf Links, rated the number one public course: Samuel F. B. Morse, Class of 1908. The namesake of his great uncle who invented the telegraph, Morse was born in Newton, Massachusetts. His mother Clara was an acclaimed artist. He studied painting in Boston and attended Phillips Andover Academy before going to Yale. He was a halfback and captain of an undefeated Yale football team and was named to two Walter Camp All-American teams. Upon graduation in 1908, the father of one of his college friends gave him his first job, working on a farming and irrigation project in the San Joaquin Valley of California.

By 1915 Morse had a new job as the manager of the Pacific Improvement Companies properties on the Monterey Peninsula. These included the Hotel Del Monte that had been built in 1879, a golf course added to the grounds in 1890, and a new real estate development called Pebble Beach, with a seventeen-mile drive through forest, valley, and shoreline totaling 18,000 acres. The owners of the Pacific Improvement Company were the leaders of Western railroading, Charles Crocker, Collins P. Huntington, Mark Hopkins, and Leland Stanford. They were disappointed by the slow sale of lots at Pebble Beach and ordered Morse to find a buyer willing to pay $1.3 million for all of the peninsula properties.

To add value, Morse scrapped the owners' existing development plan for Pebble Beach, which was to crowd as many houses as possible along the coast. He bought back all the lots that had been sold. The owner of one lot refused to sell. Morse had a different plan for development: "The average developer of land takes a chunk of it, figures out a residential and shopping area and leaves what's left over for a golf course. I approach things a little differently. In the first place I want the whole waterfront to be set aside as a greenbelt. Then I picked a tract and said to the architects, 'Use as much as you need for a golf course and we'll put the rest into lots.'" His "vision for the property included larger homes set back from the beach and overlooking a golf course that would meander along the rocky bluff above Stillwater Cove." He wanted either Charles Blair Macdonald or Alistair Mackenzie to design the course, but the former wasn't interested and the latter was fighting in World War I. So, two local amateur golfers, Jack Neville and Douglas Grant, along with Morse, designed the Pebble Beach Golf Links. Later Morse himself redesigned the par 4 eighteenth hole to make it a par 5. The course and the adjacent Lodge opened in 1919. That same year, Samuel Morse convinced his employer to sell the entire property to him and several San Francisco financial backers for the $1.3 million, the same price that no one had been willing to pay before these improvements.

For the next fifty years Morse remained the owner of the Del Monte Properties Company, the firm he formed to operate Pebble Beach. Not a tree could be cut or any kind of building erected without company approval, which meant Mr. Morse's approval. Eventually four public courses were built, as well as a private course, for which Morse did secure the services of Dr. Alistair Mackenzie. Seth Raynor had been hired to design the private Cypress Point Club course and had completed a routing plan when he died in 1926. Using that plan, Mackenzie completed the design and supervised the construction of the course that opened in 1928. Samuel Morse became an inseparable part of one of the most strikingly beautiful areas of the California coast. At age eighty he received the award of which he was proudest: Outstanding Citizen of the Monterey Peninsula of 1965. On that occasion, his son, the painter John Morse, toasted his father as "an artist who spent a lifetime painting a 20,000 acre canvas."

In 1978, nine years after his death, the property was sold for $72 million. In 1998 the family of the original owner sold the one building lot that Morse had been unable to repurchase in 1919 and Jack Nicklaus designed a new fifth hole on the cliff top site. In 1999, Olympic impresario and former baseball commissioner, Peter Ueberroth, and 132 of his friends and associates, including Arnold Palmer and Clint Eastwood, purchased the Del Monte properties for $820 million. It seems that Samuel F. B. Morse had more vision than his original bosses.

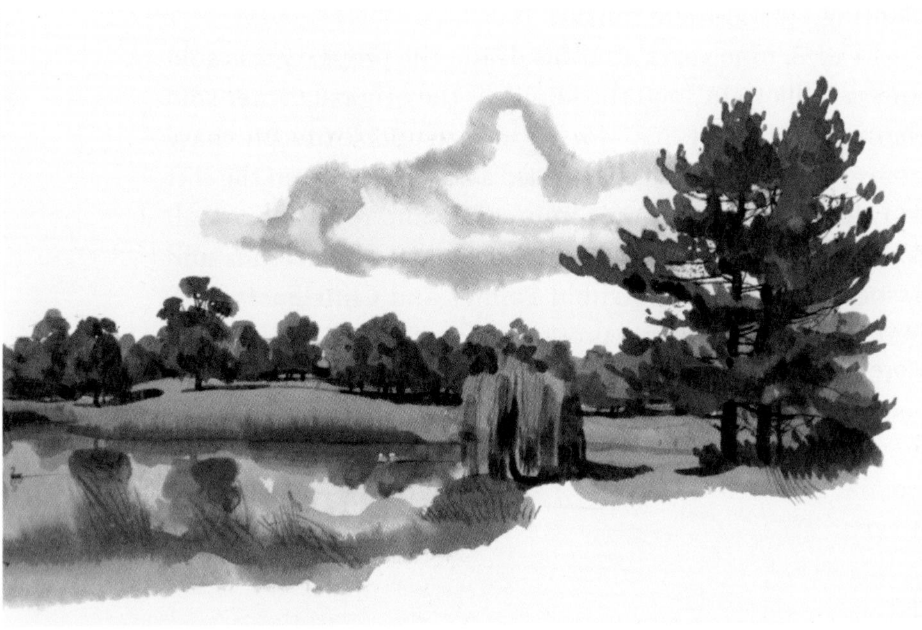

1923–1926
Building the Yale Golf Course

Yale won the first national intercollegiate championship sponsored by the USGA in 1897. Yale went on to win thirteen of the next twenty championships. Harvard and Princeton split the other seven. However, in 1922 Yale had not won for seven years. Late in 1922, George Townsend Adee wrote to the Director of the University's Athletic Association with a vision that was to change the course of Yale golf. He wrote from concern and frustration. More and more Yale undergraduates were taking to golf, and Race Brook Country Club was becoming so crowded that they were forced to go even further afield. The New Haven Country Club was closed to undergraduates. Even more worrisome, Princeton had had its own course, Springdale Golf Club, since 1895, and now Harvard was moving to build a course of its own and had started raising money earlier that year. It must have tweaked Adee that Harvard's opening fund-raiser was an exhibition match that pitted Francis Ouimet, 1913 US Open champion, and Jesse Guilford, 1921 US Amateur champion against Bobby Jones (then a Harvard Law School student) and none other than Yale's own Jess Sweetser.

The Site

Adee had graduated in the Class of 1895 and had been present at the beginning of Yale golf, although he himself was an All-American quarterback. As an involved alumnus, a Wall Street stockbroker, a former chairman of the US Lawn Tennis

BATCHELLER & ADEE

GEORGE E. BATCHELLER
MEMBER OF THE
NEW YORK STOCK EXCHANGE
GEORGE TOWNSEND ADEE
HENRY BATCHELLER

BROKERS

62 BROADWAY

TELEPHONES. {4220 4221 4222 4223} BOWLING GREEN

NEW YORK, December 12, 1922.

John T. Blossom, Esq.,
Yale Athletic Assn.,
New Haven, Conn.

Dear Jack;-

          Referring to our conversation yesterday about the proposed Yale
University Golf course, I believe a golf course at Yale is absolutely essential
if the University is to compete successfully with Harvard and Princeton. Princeton, as you know has a University golf course within one-half mile of the Princeton campus which is in operation today. Harvard is now raising the money to
build a golf course within easy reach of the Harvard campus , and work I under-
stand will be begun on it next summer. At Yale today 150 undergraduates have
the privilege of using the Race Brook Country Club course by paying $45.00 a year .
The Race Brook course is about 6 miles from the Yale Campus and takes about one-
half hour in the trolley car. The Race Brook Club, has in addition to 150 undergraduates, 418 Resident Members, 61 Non-Resident members, so that the course is
constantly over-crowded, and for this reason it is a very unsatisfactory place
for even 150 undergraduates to play. Many of the undergraduate golf players go to
the Shuttle Meadow course at New Britain or to one of the Bridgeport courses as
guests occasionally, because the Race Brook course is so over-crowded. No undergraduate can play on the New Haven Country Club course. In addition it seems to
me that the game of golf is growing faster than any other game in the country, and
that if Yale is going to have real athletic facilities they ought to have a modern
up-to-date Championship golf course for undergraduates as close to the campus as
possible, and preferably in the immediate vicinity of the new athletic field.
          We can get 122 acres of land on the south side of Derby Avenue and
running along the west side of the Race Brook course for $60,000. I have been all
over this tract of land and find it ideal as far as the terrain itself is concerned
for a golf course. It is fine rolling land with a brook running diagonally across
it, would need very little draining, has practically no rock and only about 15%
of it is wooded. To my mind it is too far away, as it would take 30 to 35 min-
utes in the trolley from the campus. The ideal spot would be part of the Greist
Estate, adjoining the present Yale field. Louis Stoddard can tell you who to go to
to find out if the Greist Estate would sell 120 of their 700 acres and you might
get a price and an option from the owners.

1922 letter from George Adee to John Blossom

Association, and a member of the Westchester Country Club, he had the experience and the connections to get things moving. Adee's letter proposed two options to the Athletic Association. The first was to purchase 122 acres of land in Orange, directly adjacent to Race Brook Country Club on Derby Avenue. Adee estimated land and construction costs for a course and clubhouse would be about $260,000.

But a second course in Orange would still be distant from campus, and Adee's sights turned closer to an unusual parcel of undeveloped woodland within the city limits. This was the estate of the late New Haven businessman, John M. Greist. Adee suggested that Yale try to obtain 120 acres or so of the extensive property, which actually bordered the Yale athletic fields beyond the Yale Bowl and stretched all the way out to Woodbridge. He noted that construction costs would be even higher because they would have to clear dense woods and deal with rock and ledge, but he urged the University on: "It seems to me that a modern up-to-date, 18-hole, Championship golf course would be a tremendous asset for Yale University, and would draw many of the most desirable men to the University." Within a few months, the University agreed, and as it pursued the Greist option, the project grew even grander.

The Greist estate that Adee had set his sights on was a 720-acre nature preserve that began on the north side of present-day Forest Road in Westville and stretched up to the present boundary of

Connecticut Magazine, August, 1903

Marvelwood, home of John M. Greist

Within the Marvelwood nature park

the Wilbur Cross Parkway. It was the pride of a local German-American manufacturer, John M. Greist, who had developed his company into the world's largest maker of sewing machine attachments. His main factory was on Blake Street in Westville (part of it remains across the street from the well-known dining establishment, 500 Blake Street), and he built one of the city's finest homes along Forest Road, adjacent to his friend Donald G. Mitchell. Mitchell was Yale Class of 1841 and was then one of the country's best-known writers. He wrote under the penname of Ik Marvel, which inspired Greist to name his own estate Marvelwood.

Around the turn of the century, Greist bought up all the land from their two estates northwards towards Woodbridge; almost all of the land had last been farmed in 1880 and was now largely covered by second-growth forest and inhabited by birds, wild animals, and fish in ponds and lakes. It became the second-largest protected open space in the state.

With a staff of supervisors and workers, Greist maintained it as natural woodland, not a hunting preserve. He surrounded it with seven miles of wire fence and created fifteen miles of interior paths for fire protection. The fence was not to exclude local residents, who could enter through one of seven gates and were welcome to walk the preserve. Rather, it was to keep the wildlife from crossing into the surrounding neighborhoods. Greist wanted the park to preserve the flora and fauna of New England, although, in 1905, he did introduce a small herd of elk and deer from Colorado. Unfortunately, the next year, Yale senior, Chauncey Brooks McCormick, was badly gored by an elk, and Greist thereafter closed Marvelwood to the public during rutting season.

Greist died in 1916, and the preserve remained in family hands. By the early 1920s, real estate developers were pressuring to buy it for housing for an expanding city. This must have been on Adee's mind when he made his proposal to the University, and he even had a strategy in mind that involved one of University's earliest football stars.

Ray Tompkins had been captain of the Yale football team in both 1883 and 1884, at the beginning of the long Walter Camp era. Tompkins achieved considerable financial success as the president of the Chemung Canal Trust Company in upstate New York. When he died in 1918, he left his wife an estate valued in excess of a million dollars, with the provision in his will that, upon her death, the remainder was to pass to Yale University "to furnish facilities for extending and developing the practice of athletic exercises on the part of students of the University." In early 1923, just after Adee's proposal, the University approached Sarah Tompkins to ask her to purchase the entire Greist estate as a gift to the university in her husband's memory. She readily accepted, and Yale immediately bought the 720 acres for $375,000, a much lower figure than the real estate developers had offered. When Yale President James Angell accepted the gift and designated the property as the Ray Tompkins Memorial, he emphasized its use for "recreational sport first and competitive athletics next: i.e., the golf course, natural outdoor swimming pools, gun club ranges, cross country courses and similar developments." Later it was announced that the Memorial was to be used "in the development of an out-of-doors program of sports including tobogganing, skiing, skating and tramping." Finally, 200 acres were set aside as a preserve for native plant and animal life at the request of Dean Harry Graves of the School of Forestry.

A Yale Golf Committee was quickly formed, with George Adee as chairman. Other alumni members were J. F. Byers (at the time, president of the USGA), R. A. Gardner (then serving as USGA vice-president), and the former USGA treasurer, M. N. Buckner. Junior student Jess Sweetser and John T. Blossom, the Graduate Director of Athletics, represented the University. Jess Sweetser told David Paterson in a 1989 interview that he was the one who suggested that the committee consult with Charles Blair Macdonald to confirm his view that the land had "beautiful potential." Sweetser had a deep admiration for Macdonald from playing several of his courses, especially Lido on Long Island. Correspondence indicates that Adee himself approached his good friend Macdonald. Macdonald, then sixty-eight, had "renounced having anything to do with

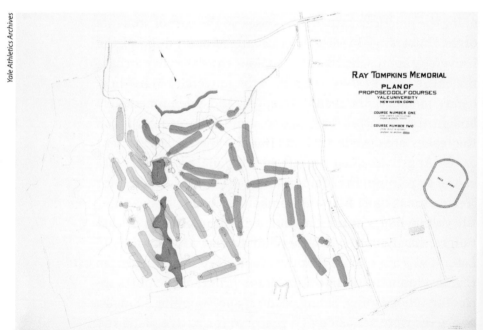

Yale Athletics Archives

Seth Raynor's original 1924–1925 design for two 18-hole layouts. The layout in light green was the one that was actually built.

building another golf course," but he agreed to serve as a consultant and immediately recommended that the committee hire his former associate, Seth Raynor, as the architect. Raynor was duly hired at his usual fee of $7,500. He spent the summer of 1923 surveying the entire property and, by the fall, had completed a design for two eighteen-hole courses and a cost estimate for building the first.

Thus, the Yale course was fashioned by two of the most important figures in golf at the time — Charles Macdonald, the first national champion golfer and the American father of golf course architecture, and Seth Raynor, a non-golfing engineer whom Macdonald had brought into the course design business and who had deeply imbibed the tutoring of his mentor to become successful in his own right.

Charles Blair Macdonald
The course design consultant

Charles Macdonald was born in Canada of naturalized American parents, a Scottish father and a part Mohawk Indian mother. In his magnificent biographical study, *Evangelist of Golf* (Clock Tower Press, 2002), George Bahto describes how Macdonald grew up in Chicago and was educated at St. Andrews University in Scotland in 1872-74, where he learned to play golf from Old Tom Morris himself. He became a successful stockbroker in Chicago but had no opportunity to continue his golf until 1892, when he and several friends built a basic nine holes in anticipation of a visiting English delegation to the 1893 World's Columbian Exposition. Macdonald expanded it to a more substantial eighteen-hole course the following year. In 1894, he competed in two "national championships" that were held first at Newport and then at St. Andrew's. He finished runner-up in both and created a stir by complaining vociferously about the formats and rulings. The

Charles B. Macdonald,
circa 1922

result was the formation of a United States Golf Association at the end of the year by representatives of leading clubs, and Macdonald proceeded to win its first official US National Championship in late 1895.

However, Macdonald's true genius was in "golf architecture," a term first used by him, and the design of courses became his avocation. Faced with still rather crude and unchallenging courses in the United States, Macdonald's key insight and central principle was to elevate the American game by adapting the "best holes" and best strategic elements of famous British Isles links. Several trips across the Atlantic and careful surveys allowed Macdonald to develop a course aesthetic and a design vocabulary that he applied forcefully and creatively to New World topography. In 1908, he began a project that would result in his "ideal golf course," the National Golf Links of America on Long Island. He engaged a local Southampton surveyor-engineer, Seth Raynor, to draw up the detailed plans, which was the start of an enormously significant partnership. Raynor was a non-golfer (and largely remained so the rest of his life), but he immediately understood Macdonald's intent and helped to devise the construction strategies to put them into effect. The National Golf Links, which first opened in 1910, and the Lido Club, which was completed in 1918 and is now defunct, were his two greatest monuments, but he was involved in the design of more than a dozen other memorable courses. He was a friend and social equal of his clients, a member of the same clubs. He staunchly believed in an "amateur" ethic and refused to accept any fees for his work. His ego was as outsized as his vision for American golf. He had a volatile temper, but no one doubted his passion for the game and his drive for perfection. There were others in that first generation of American architects who would design more courses and who are held in greater reverence, but it was he who established in America the standard that great golf demanded great courses and that the brilliance of a course was its ability to pose challenges to all who played it.

Seth J. Raynor
The course architect

At the time of his Yale course commission, Seth Raynor had already designed and/or built sixty-six courses in sixteen years, from Bermuda to Hawaii and from Minnesota to Puerto Rico — an astonishing record for someone who had stumbled into the profession by coincidence. He was not without any golfing experience when C. B. Macdonald engaged him for the National Golf Links of America in 1908. Raynor had grown up in Manorville on Long Island, and, in 1891, his father was hired to survey the land on which the Shinnecock Hills Golf Club was to be built. Seventeen-year-old Seth went along to carry the rods and chains. In 1898 he graduated from Princeton University, with a degree in civil engineering and geodesy, and he married a local Southampton girl, Mary Araminta Hallock. By 1908 he was serving as the Southampton village engi-neer and street commissioner. He also had a private business as landscape engineer and surveyor from his home office on Bow-den Square.

As George Bahto and others have written, Macdonald found Raynor a modest and reticent man. With no pre-conceived ideas about golf, he was a perfect subordinate for the demanding

Seth Raynor, circa 1925

Macdonald. And Macdonald certainly was an authoritarian. When he realized that Raynor had much more to offer than surveying, he expanded his responsibilities to supervising the actual course construction. Thus began a profitable and productive relationship of design teacher and eager and adept protégé that continued through the Yale course plans.

In 1914, as their massive Lido project began, Raynor followed Macdonald's urging and started his own golf architecture firm. Macdonald wrote in *Scotland's Gift-Golf*, "I had given him all my plans and only occasionally was I asked for advice." Raynor closely followed his mentor's design philosophy, while riding the new wave of popularity and demand for courses. In 1920, Raynor moved his office to Manhattan, and soon enlisted the help of Ralph Barton (Dartmouth 1903), brought in from the University of Minnesota, and Charles "Josh" Banks, Yale class of 1906. Raynor had met Banks, who was an English teacher at the Hotchkiss School, when he was supervising the construction of the school's golf course. Banks was so intrigued by the project that he resigned his Hotchkiss position and joined Raynor's firm. The firm often collaborated with the Olmsted step-brothers and with Frederick Ruth, who were among the most influential landscape designers and land developers of the 1920s.

The only record we have of Seth Raynor's vision of ideal course design is from a 1918 interview that appeared in the monthly magazine of the Olympic Club in San Francisco. There he stated that the optimal course should have four short holes ranging 130 to 220 yards, six drive-and-pitch holes ranging 310 to 375 yards, and eight full-shot holes ranging 400 to 540 yards, for a total length of 6,200 yards. Throughout his career he favored the replication of the great holes that he had learned from Macdonald. That well describes the Yale Golf Course in 1926 and today.

Construction began in the summer of 1923, even as Raynor was surveying the estate. By July, the C. W. Blakeslee Company had cleared and plowed approximately 100 acres of trees, stumps, underbrush, and loose rock. Almost three-quarters of this was ledge and swamp, difficult work that required blasting, filling, draining, and recovering with sand, earth, and humus to make viable soil. Macdonald himself captured some of the difficulty:

> The building of it was a difficult engineering problem. The land was high, heavily wooded, hilly, and no part of it had been cultivated for over forty years. There were no roads or houses upon it. It was a veritable wilderness when given to Yale .... When in the timber one could not see fifty feet ahead, the underbrush was so thick. However, we found on the high land wonderful deposits of sea sand, indicating that the sea must have swept the land during the glacial period. In a bog some quarter of a mile long we found deposited some four to six feet of wonderful rich black muck. These two deposits of sand and muck made it possible to build the course.

With the ponds and water courses, a total of 120 acres of the vast property was made available for the course.

Heavier construction began in April 1924, with a force of sixty laborers, which later increased to a maximum of 150. The workers were both local day laborers and men with experience in handling woods and rock who came down from New Hampshire. During summer vacations, this group was augmented with many Yale students and a few from Dartmouth. The out-of-towners were put up in three bunk houses, which adjoined a cook house and a log cabin office that overlooked Greist Pond next to the ninth green. Raynor periodically visited the construction site, but he left daily management in the hands of Charles Banks. The land clearing was managed by William Nugent, and the course construction was initially overseen by

John Czenkus, a day laborer on the project

Ralph Barton. Later William E. Perkins (Yale '17S) took over supervision.

Some of the construction details hint at the huge engineering challenge. Water was drained from the course through 3.2 miles of ditches that were dug alongside the fairways at a width of two feet and depth of three feet. Water for irrigating the greens and fairways was fed by gravity-flow through 35,000 feet of pipe that ran from a 75,000-gallon tank that was mounted atop the highest hill behind the seventh green (which abuts the present Wilbur Cross Parkway). Remnants of both the ditches and the irrigation pipes can be seen today, especially on the eleventh and seventeenth holes. After 2,850 tons of manure and 190 tons of limestone had been spread on the course and harrowed in, seed was planted on the greens and fairways in the fall of 1924. The greens were seeded with German Bent and New Zealand fescue, the fairways and tees with New Zealand fescue and Rhode Island Bent. Sheep fescue was sown in the rough.

Such a massive project required a large budget. By June 1924, the clearing alone had cost $90,000, and the Golf

*Charles Banks in **Mischianza**, the Hotchkiss School yearbook, circa 1925*

Committee asked Raynor for a revised cost estimate. His new figure for completing only the first eighteen-hole course was $251,000. The committee must have been concerned; it went ahead but began to develop a special fundraising membership program at two levels: "patron" ($1,000 for unrestricted lifetime access) and "life member" (lifetime access limited only by undergraduate tee time priority at $750 for those within twenty-five miles of the course and $500 for those beyond that range). Even without advertising, forty-four patrons signed on by January 1925, and the committee had hopes of eventually attracting at least 400 patrons. Success of the patron program could have financed the full thirty-six-hole plan. Unfortunately, the committee plans ran afoul of the University, which was beginning its own endowment campaign and feared the simultaneous competition. As a result, it absorbed all of the construction costs into its general budget, but this is likely the reason why the second eighteen-hole course was never begun.

William Perkins, circa 1950

A few selected alumni played the course in the fall of 1925 and gave it rave reviews. From the "Long" tees, the course played to a par 71 at 6,552 yards; from the "Regular" tees it was rated as par 69 at 6,061 yards, and par 69 from the "Short" tees at 5,548 yards. The fourth and sixteenth holes were par 5's from the "Long" tee, and par 4 from the other tees. Today the fourth is a par

Mixing loam, 1925

Yale Athletics Archives

Constructing the ninth hole (Worker dormitories and cook house are to the left.)

4 and the sixteenth a par 5 from all three tees, so that the course has a standard par 70. Because of the cost overruns, only a very modest clubhouse was built, with a budget of approximately $5,000. It was a "log cabin style" with two rooms on either side of a double fireplace. One side was the pro shop, and a changing room with a single shower was on the other side of the fireplace.

The committee engaged Bernard "Ben" Thomson, the professional at the Mount Kisco (New York) Club, to start his duties at Yale in March 1926, where he remained for nine months of the year. He was a Scotsman who had been wounded in World War I as a member of the Black Watch Brigade. Bill Perkins was named course superintendent and remained in that position for a quarter of a century until 1951.

Only the front nine was available for play when the course opened without fanfare on April 15, 1926. The

Yale Athletics Archives

Spectators at the site, 1925

back nine was finished shortly after, but the record is unclear about whether this was in time for the course's first intercollegiate match, played on April 24, when Yale defeated the US Army Military Academy 9-0. Early excitement was provided by Yale freshman, George Coe Graves II, who scored Yale's first hole-in-one with a mashie shot on the 135-yard, number five "Island" hole.

The eleventh hole during construction in June, 1924 (left, William Perkins; right, Seth Raynor)

The eleventh hole today

It would be another year before an exhibition was held at Yale, when, for $1.15, anyone could follow Tommy Armour, the US and Canadian Open champion, and Johnny Farrell, holder of six major titles, as they defeated Bobby Andrew, the pro at the New Haven Country Club, and Ben Thomson, 3 and 2. After the match Armour gave a special exhibition of shot-making for the gallery and then submitted to an interview for the *New Haven Register*. The paper reported his view that Yale had "one of the best courses I ever played over. The greens — well, I don't know what to say. I never saw a finer set anywhere. They are simply perfect. You know I've seen a few during the past 10 years." And in 1940 Bobby Jones said, "The Yale Golf Course is a grand one all right — got every shot in the game. It certainly ought to be the best test for your intercollegiate matches." Sixty-five years later, it is again rated as the number one university course in the country.

Sadly, the Yale course was one of Raynor's final projects, and he never lived to see its opening. Throughout 1925, he combined periodic visits to New Haven with extensive travel to other ongoing commissions. He designed Puerto Rico's first course at Berwind and was contracted to design Cypress Point in California. He was also spending time in Hawaii laying out two courses and was even scheduled to go to Japan. Raynor's grand niece describes that time, "It was too much travel, too much work, too little relaxation at West Neck (his Long Island home). Although weak from his frenzied schedule, he returned from Hawaii and immediately boarded a train to Florida. There he was expected to celebrate the opening of the second nine of the Palm Beach's Everglades Club." Sadly, he had contracted pneumonia on the West Coast, and it had worsened by the time he reached Florida. Raynor died in Palm Beach on January 23, 1926, at age fifty-one.

In less than two short decades, Seth Raynor had designed and/or built more than 100 golf courses. At his death, he left more than thirty additional courses unfinished, which Charles Banks gradually completed over the next five years. In his own work, Banks continued the Macdonald/Raynor tradition of adapting famous holes in each project. He was known as "Steam Shovel" Banks for his use of heavy equipment in moving massive amounts of earth to create huge elevated greens and deep bunkers. This too was an engineering innovation that Macdonald and Raynor had brought to course construction in the mid-1910s. Like Raynor, Banks died tragically young of a sudden heart attack at age forty-eight. Shortly before he died he wrote detailed descriptions of each hole of the Yale Golf Course, which are reprinted in a later section, "The Course, Hole by Hole."

Who designed the Yale course?

C. B. Macdonald or Seth Raynor? Over the years, the Yale community and the American golfing world have debated who should receive credit for the design of the Yale Golf Course, but the documents of those times and the weight of subsequent opinion are quite clear. Recommended by Macdonald, Seth Raynor was the architect and builder, brilliantly shaping every hole with the principles he had learned from his mentor and sponsor. On this the Yale Golf Committee was clear in its final report to the University on February 22, 1926,:

> The Golf committee was fortunate and privileged in having the advice and counsel of Mr. Charles Blair MacDonald [sic] in the preparation of its plans and in the design and laying out of the course. The late Mr. Seth J. Raynor was engaged as architect and builder.
>
> The committee put the entire 700 acres of the Memorial at the disposal of the architect and asked him to lay out 2 outstanding championship golf courses.

Writing in the *Yale Alumni Weekly* on April 19, 1929, Raynor's subordinate and successor, Charles Banks (whose byline identified him as "'06, Golf Architect"), describes Raynor's approach.

> *Raynor wormed his way through woods and thick underbrush over land strewn with boulders and covered with ledge rock. He picked his way through swamp areas, finally to emerge with a picture in his imagination of what is today considered by many to be the outstanding inland golf course in America. Mr. Macdonald was familiar with the plans from the outset, but Mr. Raynor was the real genius of this masterpiece, who made the layout, designed the greens, and gave the work of construction his supervision from start to finish.*

Yet it is equally clear that Yale was very special to Macdonald and that whatever designs Raynor (and Banks and Barton) so brilliantly executed in transforming this rugged nature expressed the philosophy that Macdonald had firmly held and clearly articulated for a quarter of a century. He was indeed "the evangelist of golf" for the New World, as George Bahto demonstrates, and Raynor was his acolyte. When Macdonald wrote his autobiographical *Scotland's Gift-Golf* in 1928, he lavished his attention and memories on only four courses: National, Lido, Mid-Ocean, and Yale. It was a natural progression. He had designed the first two himself, as capstones of his design beliefs. He had laid out Mid-Ocean jointly with Raynor and had enthusiastically left Raynor with full control over the Yale project. He was proud of his protégé's result, boasting in his autobiography that "To-day Yale has a classical course, which is unexcelled in comparison with any inland course in this country or Europe." He would be pleased to know that, eighty years later, the course remains so highly regarded. So too is Macdonald. In 2007, he was inducted into the World Golf Hall of Fame.

1926–1943
The Ben Thomson Era

Bernard "Ben" Thomson
Yale Golf Course professional and team coach

Ben Thomson was born in Scotland, where he served his apprenticeship as a golf club maker and amateur player. He fought and was wounded in World War I while serving with the Black Watch Third Battalion of the Royal Regiment of Scotland. After the war he came to this country as a golf professional, working at Southampton, Aiken, and Mt. Kisco before coming to Yale in March 1926 as the first professional at the new course.

From the beginning, the new course and Ben Thomson were great successes. By 1927 there were 435 student members of the golf club. The university golf team was chosen from the twelve players with the lowest scores in the University Championship tournament, which was played in the spring. These twelve student golfers played another eighteen holes, and the eight players with the lowest scores made the team. Only six players could compete in tournaments, so Coach Thomson always allowed the number seven and number eight players to challenge the number five and number six players for competition spots. As Thomson said, "In this way the interest is kept up among the players, which means that the whole squad is constantly practicing to perfect their game and keep their place on the team."

Competition must have been intense because the 1927 University Championship had 100 entrants, twenty of whom

© Prentice-Hall, Inc.

Coach Ben Thomson, circa 1930

scored under 84, four scored under 80, and three, under 76. Lewis Parker beat Ben Thomson's course record of 74 by a stroke. That same year Thomson took part in the first exhibition at the course to raise money to support the golf program. He and Bobby Andrew, the New Haven Country Club pro, lost to Tommy Armour, US and Canadian Open Champion and Johnny Farrell, the holder of six titles. Tickets were $1.15 (including tax) and included the match and a special exhibition of shot-making by Tommy Armour after the match.

The golf team continued to win the national intercollegiate championship with regularity. The team won in 1926, 1931, 1932, 1933, and 1936, and Tom Aycock won the individual national championship in 1929. Ben Thomson reported in the *Yale Alumni Weekly* in 1931 that on average 150 students per day were playing the course and that freshman L. Weatherwax had lowered the course record to 66.

By the 1930s intercollegiate golf was becoming truly national. Michigan won the national championship in 1934 and 1935, and Stanford took it in 1938. In the midst of Yale's dominance, in 1931, it joined with Brown, Dartmouth, Georgetown, Harvard, Holy Cross, Penn, Princeton, and Williams to form the Eastern Intercollegiate Golf Association (EIGA), so even in years when it didn't qualify for the national championship it could play for the EIGA Maxwell Cup. Yale won every EIGA championship from 1931 to 1938.

Thomson was the first coach to take the team abroad. In 1937 they toured England and Scotland and played at St. Andrews. The team included Sherwood Munson, Ed Meister, and Fred Borsodi, each of whom later gained distinction. In 1939, Ben Thomson published an instruction book, *How To Play Golf*. In his words, it was for *"people who want to take up golf under some guidance, but cannot afford to pay the cost of instruction from a competent professional .... To make the game pleasant and easy — as, in fact, it is — is the goal of instruction, and to that end this book is dedicated."* Most of the illustrations in the book are photographs of Joe Sullivan, then Thomson's assistant, demonstrating the important points of instruction. The book went through five printings.

Throughout his tenure, Thomson worked with Superintendent Bill Perkins to improve the course. In 1929 he reported to the Athletics Department that *"large new tees have been placed at the first, fourth, fifth, seventh and ninth tees on the outward nine and at the eleventh, fourteenth, fifteenth, sixteenth and eighteenth on the inward nine. The rough and swamp immediately in front of the 18th tee has been all cleared away from this beautiful hole making it easier for the player who should be unfortunate enough to miss a drive, where a good one is necessary."*

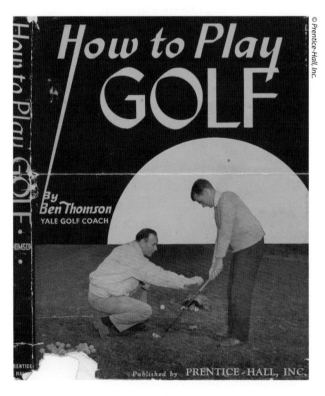

Yale won the EIGA championship again in 1942 and took what was to be its last national championship in 1943. Sadly, Coach Thomson was not present for either event. In March 1942, the outbreak of war led the Yale Athletic Association to begin a retrenchment program and it fired Thomson along with the tennis and baseball coaches and the veteran director of athletics publicity. Thomson had served the University for seventeen years, the tennis coach had been there for twenty-eight years, and Smoky Joe Wood, famous as the pitching ace of the 1912 World Champion Boston Red Sox, had coached Yale baseball for twenty years. Ben Thomson responded by taking his teaching enthusiasm into service and joined the Air Corps as a machine-gun instructor.

Paul Haviland
1927 team captain

Paul Haviland (Class of 1927) began and ended his golfing career at Brooklawn Country Club in Bridgeport. At Yale he was a member of the intercollegiate champion teams of 1925 and 1926 and he captained the 1927 team.

After graduation Haviland continued winning. In 1927 he broke the thirty-six-hole qualifying record, set by Jerry Travers in 1906, when he shot 143 in the 27th Metropolitan Amateur Championship. Later that summer he won the Connecticut Amateur Championship played at the Greenwich Country Club. Haviland's success continued the next year when he defeated Max Marston, a former national amateur champion, in the finals of the Shenecossett Golf Club Invitational. He won the New England Amateur Championship in 1929, but a year later he was dead at the age of twenty-five.

Paul Haviland's friends organized a memorial tournament, open to all players from the Eastern Intercollegiate Golf Association, and played at Yale for the first time in June 1931. The

The 1926 golf team that won the national championship. From left: William K. Lanman, Jr., William K. Child, George H. Flinn, Jr., Frank E. Wattles, Paul Haviland, Lewis Parker

Yale Athletics Archives

tournament attracted a large and competitive field for several years, but it did not continue after World War II.

Milton Pierpont "Pipie" Warner
National championship team member

"Pipie" Warner (Class of 1933), as he was known around Yale and his Pine Orchard home in Branford, Connecticut, represented Yale in the 1932 and 1933 National Intercollegiate Championships and helped them win both team events. Warner pulled off a surprising win in the 1932 North & South Amateur Championship at Pinehurst, North Carolina (first played in 1900) by beating a former Yale golf star, John B. Ryerson (Class of 1921) by 5 and 3 over the thirty-six-hole final. Warner started his title quest by beating Chandler Harper (who later turned pro and won the 1950 PGA

Championship) 2 and 1 in the first round, team-mate J. E. Parker by 3 and 2 in the quarter-finals, and Jimmy Robbins in the semi-finals 2 and 1.

Remaining in form, Warner won the second Paul Haviland Cup in 1932 with a thirty-six-hole score of 149, again helping Yale to win the team championship.

Frederic A. Borsodi
Varsity golfer and wartime test pilot

When Fred Borsodi (Class of 1939) left Texas for Yale in the fall of 1935, he was already an amateur road racer (in a Grand Prix Bugatti) as well as a golfer. His most memorable Yale golf experience was losing the student University Championship to freshman Eddie Meister in the spring of 1937. Later that year the team traveled to Scotland, and he tied the course record of 69 at the Old Course of St. Andrews while competing in The West of Scotland Golfer's Alliance Open Championship.

Borsodi had learned to fly and became an avid aviator with the Yale Aero Club, which maintained planes and hosted competitive intercollegiate air shows at the local New Haven airfield. This led him to join the Navy as a pilot after graduation, but he resigned after one year, got married, and went to work for the Chance-Vought Company as a test pilot. The December 7, 1941 attack on Pearl Harbor changed his mind again. John Field (Class of 1937) related Borsodi's actions in his book, *The War Begins*:

> *The young man in civilian clothes appeared at the Army Air Corp base at Windsor Locks, Connecticut, three days after Pearl Harbor. He said he knew how to fly and wanted to join the Air Force. Assigned to check him out was Lt. Waldo Johnston, Yale 1937, base operations officer. Waldo got into the front seat, the applicant in the back of an AT-6. Off they went to go through the routine figure eights, pylons, and so*

on. "He went through the book maneuvers flawlessly," remembered Waldo. "Then, just as we were preparing to land, he asked me if I'd mind staying up a little longer. He'd like to try this plane out a bit. I said, 'Sure.' God almighty, in the next half-hour I was put through something like I've never been put through before or since. We rolled and plunged and cartwheeled and skipped and danced. We even went down under the trees along the Farmington River. Right side up, upside down, it made no difference to him. [Ed. note: At Yale, Fred had been a tumbler on the gymnastics team and a diver on the swimming team, in addition to his golf.] I'd never seen such a pilot, but I was damned if I was going to say I'd had enough. I stuck it out. When I landed, shaking, I told him blandly, 'I think you're capable of flying this plane.'"

Barbara Borsodi Gilbert

Frederic Austin Borsodi (left) with Hector Thompson, 1937 British Amateur Champion (right)

Waldo was right; Fred flew 130 combat missions in Europe and North Africa. In 1943 he was shot down and lived to tell about it in a letter to his Yale roommate Bill Atterbury.

Our group has been very active in the current campaign, and thus far we have seen a good bit of action. Our losses have been fairly high, but not too bad when the amount of operation time is considered. Bill Barnes is missing at the present time, apparently lost on a strafing mission about a week ago. I was knocked down on the same mission and had rather a narrow squeak. All of us were strafing the Jerry (German) and Italian advance forces, and they were throwing up extremely heavy antiaircraft fire. We usually get right, down on the deck and let all six guns go at anything in sight. On this particular occasion I was hit very 'solidly' about five or six miles over the enemy lines. The old ship caught fire right away, which was most embarrassing. I wheeled and started for home pronto, but the fire got a bit too bad before I could make it, and I had to jump. You remember how you and Tal Pearson and I used to discuss jumping and what it would be like. Well, I can say it is quite a thrill — I didn't have much time to deliberate as it was — merely the choice between getting toasted in the darned cockpit or scrambling out, so I scrambled. I was only 500 feet up when I got out, but the chute opened right away, I swung back and forth about twice and kerplunk! — landed right between the two lines. There was a helluva battle going in progress at the time and after getting out of the harness I frankly didn't know what in hell to do so I just lay there. Finally a little New Zealand tank scurried out and picked me up. I jumped in and off we streaked to safe ground with Jerry popping at us all the time. The tank would break down at a moment like this, so the crew and I got out and high-tailed it. Those last 300 yards would have made Jesse Owens proud of me. I spent the night in a slit trench with the New Zealand boys (picked up a nice batch of fleas too, incidentally) and then hummed my way back to our landing ground the following day — tired and hungry, but no worse for wear.

Forty-five years later his exploits were still remembered in this October 1988 article in the *Yale Alumni Magazine*.

A memorable flight Major Frederic A. Borsodi made in a "requisitioned" JU-88 from Italy to Wright Field. The Major, then C.O. of the Comanches, decided to pick up a bomber-type plane to transport PX supplies and ferry personnel to and from leaves. Acting on a report that the Foggia airfields were littered with damaged aircraft, three of Fred's lads set out for the town. A British 8th Army brigadier reported "jerry was all around the area," as he spoke, mortar shells started falling. The advance party found sanctuary with an Italian family from where they witnessed the tank battle and capitulation of the city.

As the 8th Army moved in, search for a bomber began. Foggia Main was explored without success, but a satellite field yielded a partly damaged JU-88 that the experienced eye of Sgt. Walderon decided could be fixed. When Fred Borsodi received word of the find, he dispatched a crew to repair the JU-88 with parts salvaged from other German aircraft in the area. Six days later, with insignia painted on and ack-ack batteries warned, Major Borsodi taxied the JU-88 three miles to a suitable runway and took off. The JU-88 was taken out of Comanches service when higher ups decided the plane should be sent to the United States as a subject for research. With 117 sorties behind him, Fred volunteered to fly the aircraft across the ocean. Colonel Bates convinced Major General James Doolittle that it was a good idea.

When Borsodi returned in 1943 to Wright Field in Dayton Ohio, it was as the Air Force chief test pilot. The US was just developing a jet fighter plane, which the Germans already were readying for combat. Lockheed built four YP-80A "Shooting Stars" in its Burbank, California factory. Two planes were disassembled, boxed, and shipped as deck cargo to Burtonwood, England in December 1944 for reassembly and testing. The first test flight on January 27 was successful, but tragically, the next day, with Major Frederic Borsodi at the controls, the plane caught fire and crashed. This time Borsodi didn't survive. He was buried with full military honors at the American Military Cemetery in Cambridge, England. During his service as a combat pilot he had been awarded the Distinguished Flying Cross with one Oak Leaf Cluster and The Air Medal with fifteen Oak Leaf Clusters.

The student University Championship, in which Borsodi had reached the final round in 1937, had been played yearly from 1896 until its suspension in 1950. In 1986, Coach Paterson, with support from the Class of 1937, resumed the tournament as the F. A. Borsodi Student Championship. Fred Borsodi's two daughters, Lindsley and Barbara, were present when the first trophies were awarded to the winners, Willis Arndt, Class of 1990, in the men's division and Marjorie Funk, a graduate student, for the women's division.

Edward L. Meister
1940 team captain and longtime amateur

Ed Meister (Class of 1940) was a golfing prodigy. At age fifteen he had reached the semifinals of the Cleveland District Championship, which he later won five times. At Yale he was undefeated as a freshman. In 1937 he was the first freshman to win the annual University Championship, when he defeated varsity player Fred Borsodi. For the next three years Meister was the number one player and captain of the varsity team in 1940. But, during that time, the team suffered a championship drought.

After graduation Meister returned to the family publishing business in Willoughby, Ohio. His father had started the American Fruit Growers Publishing Company in 1932. Meister grew the business and was president for thirty years of the company that is now know as Meister Media World-wide. For the next thirty-five years he was a prominent figure in amateur golf. He qualified for the US Amateur twenty-five times and played in the Masters Tournament three times. He reached the semifinals of the French and Canadian championships and the US Senior Amateur.

The semifinal match with Arnold Palmer in the 1954 US Amateur at Detroit was the high point of Meister's career. It was the same for Palmer's amateur career. Palmer had defeated Frank Stranahan and Don Cherry in the quarterfinals. Hearing that their son had made it to the semifinals, his parents back in Latrobe drove all night to Detroit, as Palmer himself was later to relate:

Yale Athletics Archives

While Ed Meister looks on stoically, Palmer holes the winning birdie on the thirty-ninth green in their semi-final match, 1954.

> *Mother and Pop drove all night to be there for the match with Ed Meister, a publishing executive from Cleveland whom I had beaten to win the 1953 Ohio Amateur. Boy, did they get a good show!*
>
> *I think fatigue set in early in our match. Ed and I had played six intense matches in the previous four days, so we were a little sloppy in our morning round. I held a 1-up advantage after the first eighteen, but shot 76. Things got a little better in first nine holes of the afternoon session, but in the final nine holes our adrenaline started pumping, and we both played some pretty awesome golf. All square through thirty holes, I hit one of the best shots of the week at the par-three thirteenth. The ball stopped forty inches from the cup, leaving me an easy uphill putt for birdie. But Ed rolled in a twenty-five footer for birdie ahead of me, which put a lot of pressure on my short one. I made it, but the match remained all-square.*

He did it to me again on sixteen. I was 1-up with three to play and had hit my tee shot on the par three to within nine feet when Ed rolled in another twenty-five footer for birdie. This time I missed my birdie putt, and we were tied again. It stayed that way through eighteen, where I had to make a knee-knocking five-footer to take the match to extra holes.

I thought I'd lost it on the first extra hole. Ed hit his approach to five feet and had a much easier putt to win than the one I'd made one hole before to extend the match. But his putt hit the low side of the hole and spun out. He missed another putt of sixteen feet on the thirty-eight hole, which would have ended it. It wasn't until the thirty-ninth hole — the 510 yard, par five third that I ended the match by hitting a 300-yard drive and a 3-iron second shot onto the green thirty feet from the hole. Ed struggled after his tee shot found the trees. After he left his fourth shot short, he took off his hat and conceded what turned out to be the longest semi-final match in US Amateur history at that time.

The next day Palmer defeated Bob Sweeny to win the championship. If Stranahan, Cherry, Meister, or Sweeny had won, it is doubtful that their subsequent lives would have been changed. But if Palmer had been defeated, his life and the face of professional golf during the next fifty years might have been very different. For, as he told James Dodson, this event was "the turning point in his life."

Arthur C. "Ace" Williams
1943 team captain

The Yale golf team won its twenty-first and last national inter-collegiate championship at the Olympia Fields course in Chicago in 1943. The team of seniors Bob Kuntz, J. G. Harris, Walter Beckjord, and junior Keith Bridston played thirty-six holes in a total of 614 strokes and beat second-place Michigan by four strokes. However, they played without their team captain, Ace Williams (Class of 1943), who was serving as a Marine Corps Corsair pilot in the war.

Arthur Williams had arrived at Yale in 1939 as a good enough golfer to have already won the New Jersey Junior Amateur Championship. He was elected captain of the freshman team that won all but one of its matches. One of his teammates was Bud Semple, who later became president of the USGA.

One experience from that freshman year remains vivid in Williams's memory. Bobby Jones, winner of the Grand Slam in 1930, came to New Haven as one of the first inductees into the Hall of Fame of the Connecticut Sports Writers Alliance. Arthur was trying out for the Yale Daily News staff, so he called Jones at the Taft Hotel and arranged a special interview. In the interview he

Yale Daily News

"Ace" Williams, 1943 team captain

learned that the thirteenth hole at the Yale course was one of Jones's favorites. Jones also praised the indoor practice facility that Ben Thomson had constructed in the Payne Whitney Gymnasium.

During Yale's spring break in 1940, Coach Ben Thomson welcomed golfers from all classes (who could pay their own way) on a trip to Augusta, Georgia. They played matches at Augusta Country Club, Aiken Country Club, and the Augusta National Golf Club. On the way home, they played at Pinehurst No. 2. Williams was on the trip with his fellow freshmen, who became "friends for life."

As a sophomore Williams was one of three team members who qualified for the individual competition at the 1941 NCAA National Championships. He qualified for match play with a score of 141 (as did Cary Middlecoff) but lost his second match. The 1942 team went undefeated and won the Eastern Intercollegiate Championship. That spring Williams was elected captain. Beside his commitment to academic study and the golf team he was also working for the *Yale Daily News* and logged 35 hours learning to fly in the Government's CPT program. In June 1942 Williams left for war time service.

After the war he returned to competitive golf and reached the final of the Connecticut Amateur in 1956, where he lost to Alpheus Winter (Yale 1939). Williams has qualified for the National Amateur three times. His most memorable golf experience came in the 1961 playoff to qualify for the John G. Anderson Memorial Four-Ball Tournament at Winged Foot Golf Club, Mamaroneck, New York. With club professional, Claude Harmon, looking on, Williams aced the tenth hole of the West Course (his first of six holes-in-one). Many assume this string of aces gave him his nickname, but he actually acquired it in his youth at Andover, from his initials A.C. At age eighty-six in 2008 he was still working as a lawyer, playing golf to a 16 handicap, and regularly shooting his age.

Herbert Warren Wind
Golf writer, editor, and publisher

"Herb" Wind (Class of 1937) was born in Brockton, Mass. He learned to play golf in the summers at Brockton's Thorny Lea Golf Club. Wind made the varsity teams at Yale in basketball and track and field. He covered sports for the *Yale Daily News* and he wrote on jazz for the *Yale Record*. After graduating from Yale, Wind earned a Masters of Literature degree from Cambridge University (1937-1939). While at Cambridge, Wind met the famous British golf writer, Bernard Darwin, and fell under his spell. With Darwin's vivid prose as a model, he determined to become a golf writer.

After two years active service with the Air Force in China during World War II, Wind settled in New York City. From 1947 to 1954 he was a staff writer for *The New Yorker*, during which time he wrote *The Story of American Golf*. He was the golf editor of *Sports Illustrated* from 1954 to 1959. In 1960 he helped launch the TV series, "Shell's Wonderful World of Golf" and wrote all the scripts for the shows in its first two years. In 1962, Wind returned to *The New Yorker* as its golf and tennis writer until he retired in 1989. In 1982 he co-founded "The Classics of Golf," an elegant series of reprints of the best of golfing literature from the last 150 years.

The accolades never ceased for what the sportswriter Frank Litsky described as Wind's "elegant but straightforward style that showed respect for his subject." To *The Times of London*, Wind was "America's finest golf writer." To the *New York Times*, he was "the dean of American golf writers." His narrative powers are seen in a profile of Arnold Palmer that he wrote for the "Sporting Scene" in *The New Yorker* in 1962.

Let us say he is a stroke behind, with the holes running out, as he mounts the tee to play a long par 4. The fairway is lined by some 10,000 straining spectators — Arnold's Army, as the sportswriters have chosen to call them — and a shrill cry goes up as he cuts loose a long drive, practically lifting himself off his feet in his effort to release every last ounce of power at the moment of impact. He moves down the fairway toward the ball in long, eager strides, a cigarette in his hand, his eyes on the distant green as he considers every aspect of his coming approach shot. They are eyes with warmth and humor in them as well as determination, for this is a mild and pleasant man. Palmer's chief attraction, for all that, is his dashing style of play. He is always attacking the course, being temperamentally incapable of paying it safe.

Wind is perhaps best remembered for an article he penned for *Sports Illustrated* about the 1958 Masters tournament, in

Herbert Warren Wind on the tee of the sixteenth hole at the National Golf Links of America (circa 1950s)

which he coined the phrase "Amen Corner," for the stretch from the second half of the eleventh hole, the short twelfth, to the first half of the thirteenth hole at Augusta National Golf Club. In an article for *Golf Digest* in 1984, he told the story of how he came to use this expression.

> *That 1958 Masters was a memorable one. It hinged on how Arnold Palmer, paired with Ken Venturi, played the 12th and 13th on the final day. Since the course had been thoroughly soaked by rains ... a local rule had been invoked for an embedded ball. On the 12th, a 155-yard par 3 across Rae's Creek, Palmer's iron carried over the green and embedded itself in the steep bank of rough behind it. The official evidently was not aware of the local rule and he instructed Palmer to play the ball as it lay. When Palmer did this, he holed out in 5, after missing a short putt. Then politely but*

pertinaciously, Palmer went back to the pitch mark of his tee shot. He obviously felt that the official's ruling was not correct, and elected to play an 'alternate' ball .... With that ball he made 3. At this point, no one knew whether Palmer's score was a 3 or 5. Palmer eagled 13 and while playing 15 he was informed that his official score on 12 was 3 ....That, in effect, won him the tournament [his first major professional championship] .... I felt that I should try to come up with some appropriate name for the far corner of the course where the critical action had taken place ....The only phrase with the word corner I could think of was the title of a song on old Bluebird record, that I first heard back in my college days — "Shouting in Amen Corner" ....The more I thought about it, the more suitable I thought the Amen Corner was for that bend of the course where the decisive action in the Masters had taken place .... My article, in the issue dated April 21, was called "The Fateful Corner."

In 1992, the PGA presented Wind with its lifetime achievement award. In 1995, the USGA gave him its annual Bob Jones Award for distinguished sportsmanship in golf. How appropriate this was since he said that his passion for golf had begun in his youth, when he listened to a radio program on Friday evenings with Grantland Rice and

Yale University Manuscripts & Archives

*Herbert Warren Wind in his office at **The New Yorker**, circa 1988*

Bob Jones. He got to know Jones while researching *The Story of American Golf* in 1948. Wind often said, "I love listening to Jones." He began covering the Masters in 1954 and talked to Jones at the tournament every year until Jones died in 1970.

In 2003, Wind donated his personal papers to Yale. In this collection, there is only one photograph of a professional golfer, Ben Crenshaw. Among the most interesting items are the letters that he received from such luminaries as Bing Crosby, Ben Crenshaw, Bart Giamatti, "Doc" Giffin, Ben Hogan, Dan Jenkins, Bob Jones, Mrs. Robert Trent Jones, Sr., Shelly Mayfield, Mrs. Jack Nicklaus, George Plimpton, Clifford Roberts, Gene Sarazen, Arthur Schlesinger, Jr., Harry Truman, Ned Vare, and P. G. Woodhouse.

William H. "Widdy" Neale, Jr.
Athletics Department administrator and coach

When you play the ninth "Biarritz" hole, you will notice that it is dedicated to Widdy Neale. After the round, if you visit the clubhouse dining room, you will be eating at Widdy's. So who was Widdy Neale?

William H. Neale, Jr., (Class of 1925 S), the youngest of six children, was born in Parkersburg, West Virginia at the turn of the twentieth century. He got his nickname as a youngster because he was "iddy-widdy" compared to his brother Earle "Greasy" Neale, who was nine years older. Greasy became the professional athlete, Widdy the amateur. Greasy is in the National Foundation Football and the Professional Football Halls of Fame; Widdy is in the Connecticut State Golf Association Hall of Fame.

At Parkersburg High School Widdy starred in football, baseball, basketball, and track. The football team was the state champions in 1916 and 1918, and he was named to the all-state team as quarterback in 1916 and halfback in 1917 and 1918. He did the same at Yale, but it took a while to get there. He entered West Virginia University and played varsity football as a freshman in 1919. He wanted to be a coach like his older brother Greasy, who coached at Washington & Jefferson College, at Yale, and the Philadelphia Eagles. Neale and his brother thought his chances of landing a good college coaching position would be enhanced by a Yale degree. The Yale

Widdy Neale, circa 1980

admissions committee was not impressed by his course of study in agriculture and horticulture at West Virginia University and turned him down. He then asked the committee to consider a delayed transfer. He would attend Marietta College for a year, not play any sports, get straight A's, pass any entrance exam the committee chose, and then be allowed to transfer. The committee agreed, and Neale went to Marietta and then passed the French entrance exam that the committee chose for him.

In 1922 he was playing halfback on the Yale team before 50-80,000 fans in the eight-year-old Yale Bowl. The 1923 team, with Widdy and six other transfers, went untied and undefeated against the usual Ivy opponents, as well as North Carolina, Georgia, Maryland and Army. Widdy also starred in baseball and basketball until his eligibility ran out. He graduated in the 1925 S class, married his high school sweetheart, and went to work.

Neale took a position in the Firestone Rubber Company management-training program. After three years, he was called back to Parkersburg; his father was ill and he was needed to manage the family hay and grain business. His father recovered and he joined an investment firm. However this was 1929 and, with a wife and son to support, not the best time to enter the investment business. By 1932, Widdy had lost his home and moved his family to a boarding house. Then his luck turned. Yale was just starting its residential college system in 1933 and wanted an inter-college (that is, intramural) athletic program. The Athletics Department called Widdy Neale to plan and manage the program.

From 1933 until 1969, Widdy ran the intramural program, and it became the standard by which other college programs were judged. He did get to become a Yale coach. He was the freshman football coach from 1934 until 1941, and the tennis coach from 1943 until 1945. He coached the National Intercollegiate Champion golf team in 1943 and the Eastern Intercollegiate Golf Association champion team in 1954.

In 1952 Neale took on a second job as business manager of the Athletic Association when Bill Perkins died unexpectedly. One of his responsibilities was to manage the golf course, which he embraced enthusiastically. Neale had discovered golf and the Yale Golf Course when he returned to Yale in 1933. He became a very good

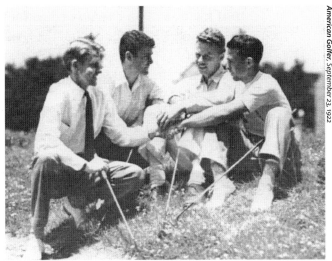

American Golfer, September 23, 1922

The last Yale team to win the National Intercollegiate Championship in 1943. From left: Keith Bridston, J. G. Harris, Walter Beckjord, Bob Kuntz

player and won the Connecticut State Golf Association Senior championship in 1946, 1947, and 1955. At age sixty-eight he still had a five-handicap. Neale was the longtime Executive

Director of the CSGA (1946-1985). He succeeded none other than Robert D. Pryde, who had served from 1899 to 1946.

During his forty-seven-year association with the Yale Golf Course, many important tournaments were held and many prominent people played the course. Nothing exemplifies Widdy's respect for the course more than the story of the most prominent person who did *not* play the course. In 1956 Widdy received a call from the White House. President Eisenhower wanted to play Yale but he had doctor's orders to use a golf cart. Widdy informed the President's representative that there were no cart paths, and that Yale golfers walked the course. Eisenhower would have to make do with Augusta National.

In 1969 Widdy Neale retired as intramural director and business manager of the Athletic Association, but he continued as CSGA executive director and assumed the position as Yale's Director of Golf. He yielded the directorship to David Paterson in 1976 but remained at the CSGA until his last year, 1985. For a good part of the twentieth-century, Widdy Neale was "Mr. Amateur Golf" in Connecticut. He was the "court of last resort" for rules questions. In 1954, the William "Widdy" Neale Scholarship Fund was established by the CSGA. By 2006, 460 caddies and other golf club workers had received $2.1 million for their college education. In 1976, Yale dedicated the famous ninth hole to him, and his name now graces the dining room in the clubhouse.

Harry Meusel
Yale Golf Course superintendent

No one has served Yale golfers longer than Harry Meusel. Like so many other of his time, he learned the game as a caddie at the New Haven Country Club. He could walk there from his home in Hamden and play in the caddie tournaments on Mondays. Just out of high school, he was drafted and assigned to Fort Dix in New Jersey to serve as a translator for German POWs. However, his superior officer was more interested in his knowledge of golf. He sent Meusel to Rutgers University to take courses that he could use in his new assignment of maintaining the Fort Dix golf course. After discharge Meusel went to the University of Massachusetts on the GI Bill to study horticulture, which became a life-long passion.

Upon graduation, Meusel interviewed for three superintendent jobs, at Race Brook Country Club, Woodbridge Country Club, and Yale. His first impression of the Yale course was that its grandeur was "unreal," and he quickly took the job offered by Bill Perkins, the business manager of the Athletics Department. Perkins had been the Yale construction manager of the course from 1924 to 1926, and superintendent of all the athletic field crews from 1926 to 1945. Meusel replaced Tony Longo, who had been the first fulltime superintendent of the golf course. Perkins challenged Meusel to make "our unique course the most beautiful golf course in the world." Perkins died suddenly a year later and did not see how Harry spent forty-one years meeting that challenge.

And it was a stiff challenge, in part because the course survived in the 1950s and 1960s on a very limited budget and a skeletal staff consisting of Harry and a six-man crew. They had a single tractor and several gang mowers that were pulled behind it. Despite sixteen-hour days during the season, Meusel later recalled, they still couldn't keep up with proper fairway and greens cutting. The rough received attention once a month, and watering was often by hand or from hoses run from wells that Harry dug in several places to supplement the original water tower.

Yet, the course landscape offered numerous possibilities to a horticulturalist like Harry. He wrote that the course was built in "second-growth woodland: beech-hemlock on the northern slopes of the rolling, rocky land and oak-hickory on the southern slopes." What now forms the second, fourth, fifth, sixth, fifteenth, and sixteenth fairways was know locally as "The Big Swamp," surrounded by gigantic tulip trees. The woodlands teemed with deer, bear, wildcats, foxes, raccoons, and small mammals. Greist Pond, the water-carry for the ninth hole, was popular for ice skating, swimming, and fishing. Both permanent and migrating birds abounded. The pond and swamp were rich in fish and water life. Mink and muskrat flourished along the edge." Harry saw that his challenge was not only to preserve the natural features, but also consciously to cultivate their great potential. He wrote, "Dogwood and laurel are naturally abundant throughout the wooded areas. By clearing away competitive growth, pruning the desirable trees, and cutting back scraggly laurel, we within a few years unlocked beauty that draws even sight-seeing non-golfers. Azalea and rhodo-dendron have been introduced around the clubhouse, and spotted about the course, providing a splash of color when indigenous growth offers little." Meusel had learned how to re-sprout mountain laurel while working in his uncle's florist shop as a teenager, and he began taking cuttings from the mountain laurels behind the ninth green (the only place where they grew naturally) and transplanting them throughout the course. On the cliff in front and below the thirteenth tee, this required lowering one of his workers by rope over the edge. Dogwoods were planted along several fairways and thousands of daffodil bulbs on the edge of woods.

Shelley Meusel Carpenter

Harry Meusel, circa 1990

At the end of the first decade, Meusel reported to the Athletics Department business manager "Widdy" Neale:

A thorough updating of the watering system began with the elimination of an antiquated gravity-flow system, which required a man to operate a diesel engine all the time the pump was running. In 1957, an electric pump and pressure tank were installed on the shore of the ninth hole pond. It is now possible to operate more than twice as many sprinklers at one time. In 1960, the third hole pond was made available as a reserve water source by connecting it to the ninth hole pond with an underground piping system. By the withering end of the 1964 season, the third hole pond was drained dry, and the ninth reservoir had receded to the critical level of the foot valves. The drought also left the seventeenth and thirteenth hole ponds cavities of sun-parched mud. We seized the opportunity to have shallow, spring-fed, pond-beds dredged to increase their water storing capacities. By means of underground pipe they were connected to one another, and the seventeenth was joined with the third. Thus the water supply in the ninth hole reservoir can now be augmented from three reserve sources.

Where the fourth fairway was once scarcely playable in the spring months, it is now kept dry by draining the third hole pond in winter, thereby lowering the water table. Because of excessive wet soil conditions, the third green was particularly vulnerable to disease. The green was raised and rebuilt with a perched water table, and it no longer poses special problems of maintenance. By 1960, every tee and green was finally equipped with a snap-valve irrigation system. Ten years ago, each green required 200-300 feet of unsightly hose and many expensive man-hours of backbreaking work to keep the greens alive during the summer months. Many tees were never watered because of their distance from the water source.

Several tees have been enlarged; No. 1 from 4,000 to 9,000 sq. ft, No. 5 from 2,000 to 6,000 sq. ft., No. 6 from

1,000 to 3,000 sq. ft., No. 9 from 2,000 to 10,000 sq. ft, and No. 12 from 1,000 to 5,000 sq. ft. A new women's tee was constructed on No. 4 to eliminate the tricky carry over the water.

Bulldozing operations connected with dredging of the seventeenth hole pond presented the opportunity to do something about the awkward cliff that compounded the difficulty of the tee shot off number seventeen. The cliff was lowered 9 feet and graded into a maintainable hillside. Dredgings from the pond were used for soil cover on the hill, and for building a new seventeenth tee.

Nuisance traps have been eliminated from the first, tenth and fourteenth holes. These traps were 70-100 yards from the tees and served no other sporting purpose than to increase the handicap of the over-par golfer. Bumps and moguls on the second green were leveled off for more accurate putting. Fairways and tees are now cut three times weekly.

Of the three new storm shelters recently constructed, two have wells for drinking water. The shelter at the first tee doubles as a caddie shelter; the fifth hole shelter also serves

Yale Athletics Archives

Maintenance barn, circa 1960

*the sixteenth tee; and the eighteenth hole shelter is conven-
ient to golfers on the eleventh hole.*

*In April of 1963, the old wooden barn, crammed to the
rafters with every piece of equipment, and every machine and
tool, burned to the ground. Now we have an all-steel building,
double the capacity of the old barn, and providing us for the
first time with such common amenities as running water,
indoor toilets, central heating, a locker room with showers,
a repair shop, and an office for the superintendent.*

The labor that he lavished on the course left him impa-
tient with golfers who did not respect it. His most famous encounter came on the day that Sam Snead had appeared to play
the course. Meusel happened to be near the ninth hole green
when Snead's tee shot landed on the front side of the massive
cross-swale. The hole that day was placed on the upper rear
green, and Snead took out a wedge and pitched his ball from
the front green, taking a huge divot. Meusel immediately
rebuked him, and Snead, notoriously short-tempered, was so
angry that he stalked off the course and never returned to
finish the round!

In keeping with his plan to "eliminate all blind holes"
Meusel filled the front cross-bunker of the twelfth hole (Alps),
and replaced it with two small flat bunkers. This bunker has
now been restored to its original configuration. Over the next
three decades, Meusel continued to work on the course.
Uneven fairways were leveled. Cart paths were built. The
installation of an automated irrigation system greatly
improved turf conditions. A new tee box was built on number
three, and many other tees were expanded. He planted evergreen trees around the new number three tee, on the right
side of the fairway on number six, and between the seventh
green and eighth tee. Over time, this proved ill-advised. By
2005 these trees had grown to more than forty feet and were

depriving the turf of sunlight and water. They have now been removed as part of Scott Ramsay's renovation program.

One unique memory of Harry Meusel is preserved in the woods to the right side of the dogleg on number fourteen. There is the figure of a woods elf (a *Heinzelmenchen* in German folklore), which has been carved from a standing tree stump by his daughter, Shelley Carpenter, in 1979 as a fifty-fifth-birthday gift to her father. This was the sixth such sculpture that Shelley had made on the course in the 1970s, and it is the only one that remains today. Another reminder of Harry is by the pond below the thirteenth tee, where he built a small, beautiful Japanese-style garden, which is being restored by Scott Ramsay. Meusel developed an abiding interest in Japanese garden design, studying it in art history seminars at Yale, traveling to Japan to tour famous gardens, and lecturing about them across Connecticut. In 1960 and 1961, he served as president of the Connecticut Association of Golf Course Superintendents, and, in 1989, he was named Superintendent of the Year by that Association.

Heinzelmenchen on the edge of the fourteenth fairway

It is fair to say that Harry Meusel met the Bill Perkins challenge!

Joe Sullivan
Assistant pro, head pro, and golf team coach

The only photograph of Joe Sullivan in the Athletics Department archives shows a very serious man in a suit and tie. That doesn't fit the man, about whom great stories have been passed down through the years. He looks more comfortable in the photographs of him demonstrating shots in Ben Thomson's book, *How to Play Golf*. Sullivan was twenty years old and already an Assistant Pro at Waterbury Country Club, when his twelfth and thirteenth siblings, twins Robert and Vincent, were born in 1929. Luckily they are still here to confirm some of what we have heard.

Sullivan came to Yale as Ben Thomson's assistant in 1939. He enlisted his ten-year old twin brothers in the caddie ranks. At the time, Joe Sullivan had a two-seat Model A Ford with a rumble seat and running boards. He drove it to the course from his home across town in Fair Haven, stopping along the way to pick up as many as eight kids plus the twins to caddie. Some told their mothers that they were staying overnight with a fellow caddie, when in fact they slept in the bunker by the ninth hole in order to be first out the next morning and "go double" for thirty-six holes! By the twins' accounting, the caddies would gather behind a brick wall in the area where the cart barn now stands, waiting to be called for a loop for seventy-five cents. On the other side of the wall was the tempting hot dog stand. New kids who joined the caddie ranks were put through an initiation of being forced to go out on a loop with thick straw wrapped under their shirts and around their bodies, creating a brutally hot, four hours in the sun.

Caddies could play the course on Mondays until noon. Robert Sullivan remembers looping for Ralph Morrell, who had played the course on opening day in 1926 and continued into his 90s. Ralph Sullivan worked at the Peabody Museum and liked to collect snakes during his round. He stored them in a net sack in his golf bag until the end of the round. In addition to caddying, another brother, Tommy worked for Joe "hawking balls" from the lake between holes three and four, as well as running the hot dog stand. On one occasion he remembers Senator Abe Ribicoff tried to get a twenty-five-cent hot dog and coke for nothing because he "was a senator."

Published by Prentice-Hall, Inc., 1939

Joe Sullivan (demonstrating the proper setup in "How to Play Golf" by Ben Thomson)

Joe Sullivan liked to teach, first as an assistant, then eventually as head pro and coach. The lesson tee was located behind the clubhouse and out to the left of the third fairway for full shots. For the short game, the area between the second and fourth greens was used. Chipping practice consisted of tossing balls underhand to the hole. For bunker play lessons, he used the eighteenth hole.

The best player that brother Robert ever saw play Yale was the amateur, Billy Joe Patton of Princeton. Later Patton finished third in the 1954 Masters. Cary Middlecoff was the only player he ever saw who could drive a ball from the first tee across Greist Pond. Gary Player and Ken Venturi also played the course during the Sullivan years.

Though some students had cars, most got to the course on a trolley that stopped at Whalley and Fountain Streets. From there they walked the two miles to the course. Joe's teams won the Eastern Intercollegiate Golf Championship five times during the nine years that he was coaching. He was quite a good player himself. On five occasions, he started a round with 3's on the first five holes. He once shot 27 on the front nine, and his best for eighteen holes was 64. Sullivan is also remembered for his ability to hit over the pond to the ninth green — while kneeling.

Because of the financial demands of raising four children, Sullivan left Yale to become Head Pro at Race Brook Country Club in 1955. He retired in 1976 and passed away the next year. Because of his deep affection for the Yale Golf Course, his twin brothers spread his ashes along the fourth fairway and the third regular tee. The fourth fairway was where he had demonstrated shot making for Thomson's book.

Al Wilson
Golf team coach and head pro

Al Wilson was the freshman soccer coach at Yale from 1950 to 1960. He was also working at his trade as a tool and dye maker when Joe Sullivan left to become the professional at Race Brook Country Club in 1955. Each of the team coaches was asked if he would be willing to take the golf coaching job. Wilson was the only volunteer. Al became certified as a PGA professional by apprenticing to Sam Snead (by telephone!) over a two-year period.

Wilson's teams compiled a 90% winning record (W-136, L-14). The team won seven Eastern Intercollegiate Championships. Three of his captains — Ted Weiss, Dan Hogan, and Ned Snyder — made All-American teams. Jerry Fehr and Ned Vare were individual EIGA Champions. Today's outstanding

Yale Athletics Archives

Dan Hogan (1965 Captain), Coach Al Wilson, Ned Snyder (1966 Captain)

golf course architects, "Bobby" and Rees Jones, played for Coach Wilson. In 1963, he was elected president of the NCAA Golf Coaches Association.

New Haven Journal-Courier

Among the well-known people who played the course during Wilson's time were Ed Sullivan, Joe DiMaggio, Jackie Robinson, George Bayer, "Porky" Oliver, and Ken

1965 Yale Golfers dunk Coach Wilson after unbeaten season

Venturi. Wilson had his son Al caddie for all of these players. "Porky" Oliver didn't like the course and told Al's son that "the guy must have been drunk who designed this course." Some of the players whom his son encountered weren't so well known. There was a foursome of bookies who came up from New York City every year, bringing their own caddies, who carried a golf bag and a cooler of beer for each player. One year, when the caddies returned the bags to the trunk of the car, son Al noticed a Thompson sub-machine gun lying there. Al Wilson's son and grandson now work in golf course maintenance.

William A. "Billy" Booe
1948 team captain and PGA pro

The first Yale graduate to become a professional golfer was better known for his football career. Billy Booe (Class of 1948) was raised in Shelton, Connecticut and attended Wilbraham Academy in Massachusetts before coming to Yale. As the place-kicker on coach Herman Hickman's Yale football team, he set a record of thirty-four consecutive points after touchdown that was not broken until 2003.

Booe also played on the golf team, which he captained in 1948. The golf team won no championships from 1944 to 1949. What Billy Booe did after graduation is not known, but he played in the US Amateur for the first time in 1955. He reached the semi-final where he lost to Harvie Ward, the 1952 British Amateur Champion.

Yale Athletics Archives

In 1956 Booe became the assistant professional to Charlie Petrino at the Brooklawn Country Club in Bridgeport. He played in the Metropolitan Open that year and the following year won $1,000 in PGA-sponsored tournaments. He led 101 qualifiers in the 1958 Bing Crosby National Pro-Am tournament at Pebble Beach California. His score of 69 beat Tony Lema by one stroke. Unfortunately he didn't advance past the second round after shooting 72-79.

In 1968 Billy Booe was very much involved in the formation of the PGA Tour. The leading professional golfers of that time, including Arnold Palmer, Jack Nicklaus, and Billy Casper, became dissatisfied with their representation in the operation of PGA tournaments. They formed the American Professional Golfers (APG) and were joined by nearly all the other tournament players. Booe was chosen as the APG tournament administrator. He had been a PGA official before he joined the APG. At the 1968 Greater Hartford Open, he announced plans for a 1969 APG tournament schedule that drew most of the sponsors of the current PGA circuit at that

Billy Booe, 1948

time. Eventually the players chose to remain with the PGA when they negotiated satisfactory representation by creating a PGA Tour entity within the PGA. The APG organization ceased to exist, and Billy Booe faded from view.

Roy "Andy" Dye
Varsity golfer and course designer

Seth Raynor and Roger Rulewich worked in the shadow of their mentors, but later emerged to establish their own identities and reputations. Very few know that in addition to Pete and Alice Dye and their two sons P. B. and Perry, there was another Dye designer, Roy, who was Pete's younger brother. Roy Dye was born in the small rural town of Urbana, Ohio, where his father designed the Urbana Country Club. He attended the Asheville School before entering Yale in 1946.

Roy "Andy" Dye (Class of 1950) played on the Yale golf team that won the Eastern Intercollegiate Golf Association championship in 1949. Billy Booe captained the 1948 team. Given Dye's and Booe's later history and what we know of Coach Joe Sullivan, those must have been fun teams. One of his eight children (three are now golf course designers), his son, Roy A. Dye III, maintained, "My father truly loved Yale. He carried it with him his entire life. When he traveled to a new city or country he would look up and contact his classmates. Those relationships he established around the world influenced his life."

Dye graduated magnum cum laude from Yale as a chemical engineer. He served in the Marines before he worked for several chemical companies involved in plastics development. When he was found to have advanced colon cancer at age thirty-nine, he was without health insurance and selling chain-link fences. For the next twenty-six years, golf-course development kept him alive. According to Pete Dye, "My brother got sick with cancer and I just gave him a job working for me." Under the tutelage of Pete, Roy Dye adopted a similar "Scottish" style of architecture. He was also influenced in his design work by playing Urbana Country Club, Ballybunion, and the Yale Golf Course.

From 1969 to 1994, Dye designed courses in Ohio, Michigan, Maryland, Colorado, Texas, Arizona, Canada, and Mexico. However, Dye's dream was to be a developer, an owner and operator — to create not only a golf course, but a total golf community. His most ambitious project was developing the 9,600-acre Carefree Ranch in Arizona. But, after three years of work, he had completed only nine holes of the course and had to defer to those with more financial strength. Most of his master plan unfolded in developing Desert Mountain where there are now six Jack Nicklaus designed courses. The last course Dye designed is his best known — the Cabo San Lucas Country Club in Mexico, which opened in 1994, the year that he succumbed to cancer. His son reminisced:

> So many Dyes had to fly from so many foreign golf courses that the service had to be planned two months after Roy's death. But before the speeches and the prayers there was one urgent question — that Dyes debated for weeks with the fervor of a benediction: "Will we play golf before, or after, the service?"

Lincoln Roden III
1952 team captain

"Linc" Roden (Class of 1952) took up golf at age thirteen in 1944 at the Huntingdon Valley Country Club, Huntingdon Valley, Pennsylvania. In 1948 he was the Regional Medalist in the USGA Junior Championship and Philadelphia Amateur Champion in 1949 and 1950. At Yale he was a member of the 1951 Eastern Intercollegiate Champion team, as well as the

Individual Eastern Intercollegiate Champion. In the summer
of 1950 he had the good fortune to attend the US Open at
Merion Golf Club in Ardmore, Pennsylvania and stand next
to Hy Peskin, when Peskin took the classic black and white
photograph know as the "Hogan One Iron." That story is best
told in Roden's own words, from his book *Golf's Golden Age
1945–1954*, published in 1995.

> In the history of golf, a few US Opens stand out as even
> more momentous than the others. One was the victory of
> Ouimet over the legendary and invincible Vardon and Ray in
> 1913. The 1930 victory by Bob Jones was part of his incredible
> Grand Slam. The 1960 Open at Cherry Hills, which saw the
> changing of the guard, was won by Arnold Palmer with his
> last round 65. The 1980 Open at Baltusrol, the brilliant and
> emotional victory of Jack Nicklaus in a record 272, is a legend.
> But, the 1950 Open at Merion Golf Club in Ardmore, Penn-
> sylvania, may be the greatest of all. I'm going to tell you about
> this Open as I saw it and as we thought about it ....
>
> As the back nine of the last round began we picked up
> Hogan. He had been even par 36 going out, and he was among
> the leaders, but he was obviously exhausted and as the back
> nine wore on, strokes were slipping away .... Hogan played a
> long iron to the front edge of 17, short of the steep rise. Three
> shots later his cushion was gone, and we knew he had to par
> 18 to get into a playoff. On 18, Hogan's drive split the middle.
> Bob and I rushed to a point right behind his ball. Hogan faced
> a shot of a little over 200 yards. He had a downhill lie with a
> slight right to left factor. There was a deep fairway swale
> short of the green, and the green was crowned. The pin was
> on the right side almost behind the left edge of the right
> greenside bunker. Hogan took out a long iron and hit a perfect
> shot for the center of the green. It landed in the swale and
> bounded up on the front third of the green. Immediately
> pandemonium broke loose as everyone raced toward the

green. Two putts later Hogan had tied for the Open at 287,
seven over par, with Mangrum and George Fazio! ... Subse-
quently we heard that Hogan had been fighting leg cramps
the whole last nine.

Hogan's long iron to the 18th green, his 36th of the day,
must stand as one of the greatest shots of all time .... We
thought it was a 2-iron. We then heard it was a 1-iron, but
we didn't believe it. We didn't think it was possible to get a
one iron up that well off the downhill lie .... After Hogan hit
his great shot there was a mad gallery rush down the fairway.
Someone stole Hogan's 1-iron. Years later it resurfaced and
now resides in the USGA Museum in Golf House .... Hogan
won the 18 hole playoff with a 69 to Mangrum's 73 and
Fazio' 75.

After Linc Roden captained the 1952 golf team and was
runner-up in the Eastern Intercollegiate Individual Championship, he served in the Korean War. In 1954, after returning
from Korea, he was the Regional Medalist and reached the
fourth round of the US Amateur, won by Arnold Palmer. Since
then, his avocation has been golf as a player, writer, and advocate for the classic game. He has been responsible for the
restoration of the abandoned (for more than fifty years) third
nine at his club, Huntingdon Valley Country Club, where he
recently shot 69. In a 2001 interview, he talked about his
support for classical course maintenance and playing
conditions.

The ultimate standards and the ultimate enjoyment of
golf occur when the fairways and greens are really hard, and
when only shots struck with the proper shape and maximum
spin will stay in the fairways or stick on the greens!

But, even with proper conditions there is the problem of
the modern ball flying so far. In the interview he addressed
that problem.

How can we restore the standards the great architects intended without adding too much extra yardage to the great old courses?

It is tragic that the powers that be have allowed the great distance increases which make so many of our great courses obsolete and which so reduce the 'standard of play' the architects intended. The only practical approach, it seems to me, is to develop a golf ball which travels about as far as Hogan's '48 distances when hit by the very best players with today's equipment.

This can best be done under the auspices of the USGA, but many have suggested this idea and the USGA has not moved. Perhaps one of the golf ball manufacturers will take the initiative.

Our 'Classic' ball would have to have reduced distance and perhaps some limit on spin rates or dimple patterns. Perhaps the ball should have the old widely used dimple pattern.

Max Behr and Donald Ross proposed the same thing in the early twentieth century, and the issue remains a lightening rod for debate. In 2007, the first question put to the new chairman of Augusta National Golf Club, Billy Payne, was how he would preserve the integrity and competitiveness of Augusta when equipment rendered it defenseless. His answer was that a Masters-only ball was being considered.

Gerald F. "Jerry" Fehr
1955 team captain

In 1944, at age eleven, Jerry Fehr was caddying and playing at the Olympic View Golf Club in Seattle. Five years later he won the high school city championship. He then won the state junior championship in 1949 and 1950. He had planned to attend Stanford University, but the local alumni group recruiting for Yale won him over, and he came here on an academic scholarship.

Jerry Fehr (Class of 1955) found the Yale golf course a "great challenge." He arrived with a "scratch" handicap, but could do no better than shoot 75 in his freshman year. He learned to play a high fade (instead of a low draw), and by his senior year, shot 66. In four years the team had three different coaches: Joe Sullivan when he was a freshman and sopho-more, "Widdy" Neale when he was a junior, and Al Wilson when he was a senior. The varsity team won the Eastern Inter-collegiate Championship in 1953, 1954 and 1955. He was the individual champion in two of those years. Perhaps his greatest feat was beating Harvard's number one player, Ted Cooney, in five of five matches over four years. In the last match played at Yale, the medal scores were Cooney 68 and Fehr 66.

After graduation Fehr returned to Seattle and worked in the insurance business. But he didn't forget the team and its success in the EIGA Championship tournament, as attested by the 1958 telegram (below).

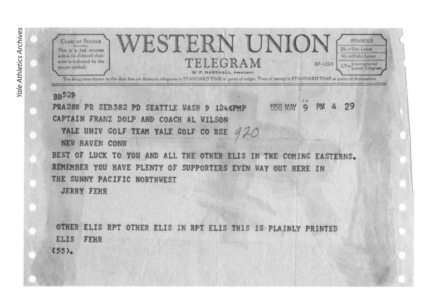

Yale Athletics Archives

He is now a member of the Sand Point Country Club in Seattle, where he has been club champion 19 times. He won the Washington State Open in 1961 and the state senior amateur in 1990. He has played in the USGA amateur, senior amateur and senior open. In 1984 he caddied for his son Rick in the US Open at Winged Foot, where Rick was the low amateur, as he had been in the Masters Tournament earlier that year.

Jerry Fehr has been involved in the Washington Junior Golf Association (WJGA) since 1982. In 1993 he became the executive director. Presently there are more than 1,000 junior golfers in the program. Those who have come to play for Yale from the program are: Ellen Brophy, Lauren Ressler, Stephanie Wei, Andia Winslow, Ashley Patterson, Greg Hull, and Ken Rizvi.

Edwin C. "Ned" Vare
1956 team captain

Like so many other sons, Ned Vare (Class of 1956) learned to play golf from his father at the Philadelphia Golf Club. But no one else could have had a mother like Glenna Collett Vare.

Glenna Collett was born in New Haven and raised in Providence, Rhode Island. There she learned to play golf from her father at the Metacomet Country Club. She became the finest female golfer of the first half of the twentieth century. In the pre-professional era from 1919 to 1959 she won fifty championships. She advanced to the finals of the US Women's Amateur Championship eight times and was the champion six times, both records that still stand. As Glenna Collett Vare and mother of two, she won her sixth US Amateur in 1935. In 1924 she didn't win the US Amateur, but she did win the Canadian championship for the second time. In 1930 she added the French championship. From 1928 to 1931 she entered and won sixteen consecutive tournaments. She was involved either as player or captain of every Curtis Cup competition from 1932 to 1950. Although Vare was never a professional, in 1953 the LPGA began presenting a trophy in her name to the professional with the lowest annual stroke average. In 1965 she received the Bob Jones Award from the USGA and in 1975 was part of the first class inducted into the World Golf Hall of Fame.

Ned Vare was also a winning golfer. In his senior year at the Episcopal Academy of Philadelphia, the golf team was undefeated and won the eastern interscholastic team championship, which was played at the Yale Golf Course. Ned won the individual championship. He played a practice round before the tournament starting on the tenth hole. On that first hole played at Yale, he scored an "eagle" by holing his 8-iron second shot. That summer he won the Philadelphia and Eastern Pennsylvania Junior Championships.

At Yale Ned Vare was captain of the freshman and varsity golf teams and also of the squash teams. The varsity golf team won the Eastern Intercollegiate Championship in 1954, 1955, and 1956. He was the individual champion in 1955, when the tournament was played at Yale. He qualified as an individual for the national NCAA tournament each of his four years at Yale. In 1954 and 1955 he played in the US Amateur Championship. He lost his first round match in 1954, but stayed on in Detroit to follow all of matches of the winner, Arnold Palmer (including the semifinal against Ed Meister, Yale Class of 1940). Vare well remembers the difficulties of the Yale course of his college years: "Any ball that missed the fairway was likely lost, as the woods came right up to the edge of the fairway."

After graduation Vare stayed at Yale to study architecture for a year and a half. He joined the Army and was discharged in 1959. That year, as an amateur with a one-stroke handicap, he Monday qualified for four PGA tournaments. During the next twenty years he followed many occupations, as school-teacher, contractor, furniture designer, ski instructor and rancher. In Tucson, Arizona in 1979, he advertised his services for "golf teaching lessons, by former PGA Tour player, at the student's own course." He became a golf pro without ever becoming a member of the PGA! Vare wrote an innovative book on the golf swing and, in 1984, returned to New Haven as a golf instructor.

David M. Ragaini
"Believe It or Not"

Dave Ragaini (Class of 1963) was a three-time letter-winner on the Yale golf team, but some say that his career highlight was a stroke he made playing on his knees to win a bet. At the 207 yard par 3 at the Wykagyl Country Club in New Rochelle, New York, Ragaini swung a 3-wood while kneeling and scored a hole in one—making it into Ripley's "Believe It or Not"!

After Yale Ragaini had additional golf achievements—standing on his feet. Most notably, in 1971, after a seven-year competitive absence, Ragaini stunned some of the Metro New York region's best professionals by taking the 49th Westchester Open Championship at the Wykagyl Country Club. At the time, he was a twenty-nine-year-old amateur who was singing commercial jingles for a living. He took on and beat, among others, former Masters and PGA Champion Doug Ford, PGA Tour star Don Massengale and Dick Siderowf, British Amateur Champion. Ragaini sank long putts to save pars on the final two holes.

Twenty years later, Ragaini, with partner Cliff Taylor of Spring Lake, Michigan, won the second National Senior-Junior Amateur at the Cobblestone Country Club in Palm City,

Florida. After a 70-67 start, they clinched the 54-hole event with an eight-under 64 scramble score.

James Gamble Rogers III
1968 team captain, clubhouse architect, and Yale Golf Association president

Jim Rogers (Class of 1968) arrived at Yale in the fall of 1963, and encountered a campus whose overall plan and most of whose Gothic revival buildings had been designed by his grandfather, James Gamble Rogers, Class of 1889 — one of the most important architects of his generation. Indeed, architecture runs through the Rogers clan. There have been six family members named James Gamble Rogers. All have been architects except Jim's father and son.

Beginning with the Yale Club of New York in 1915 and over the next twenty years, his grandfather designed most of Yale's central campus: Harkness Memorial Tower, Sterling Memorial Library, the Law School, the Graduate School, the University Theater and Drama School, and eight residential colleges. He was also the architect for five houses on fraternity row and the Bob Cook Boathouse.

The Rogers family was part of the Connecticut shoreline community of Old Black Point, and his grandfather had been a good friend of Edward Harkness, the great philanthropist who underwrote much of the Yale building program. It was a short ride from the Rogers home to the Harkness's summer estate in New London and his private golf course. Rogers's grandfather was an enthusiastic but poor golfer. He had such difficulty with sand traps that he putted out of those at the Harkness course until they were all remodeled with lips to prevent that style of exit.

Jim Rogers learned to play golf as a teenager from his father, who was not an architect but a Yale graduate. He entered Exeter in the tenth grade, where he played golf and hockey. Dan Hogan was the senior captain of the golf team when Rogers was a sophomore. In his first year at Yale Jim was a member of the undefeated freshman hockey team, but he didn't play golf. He might have avoided golf altogether had he not received a call in February of his sophomore year from Dan Hogan. Hogan had preceded him to Yale and was the 1965 golf team captain and an honorable mention All-American. Hogan suggested that he join the team for its spring trip to Hilton Head Island and Florida. Charles Fraser, Yale Law 1953, was just beginning the development of Sea Pines Plantation at Hilton Head and had invited Al Wilson to bring the team to try out the two courses that had been built. Jim Rogers turned in the lowest total score and returned to Yale as a member of the team, which went undefeated that season.

Rogers decided to leave Yale at the end of his sophomore year, frustrated that he wasn't getting from it what he thought he should. Given the Vietnam draft, he wished to remain in school and spent a year at the University of London in its School of Oriental and African Studies. Six weeks in West Africa as a teenager with his father and the Reverend Jim Robinson, founder of Operation Crossroads Africa, had stirred his interest, and he spent the year in London in the company of many of the African students at the university.

Rogers returned to Yale in 1966 and to the golf team. He

New Haven Register

James Gamble Rogers, 1968

played the number two position as a junior and the number one as a senior. In his senior year he was the runner up to Mike Porter of Princeton (now a Harvard Business School professor) in the 1968 ECAC tournament. He finished in the top twenty-five in the NCAA tournament. He followed the eventual winner, Hale Irwin, for nine holes and saw him make four birdies, four pars, and a hole-in-one. The team remained very successful, contributing to Al Wilson's remarkable coaching record. Rogers went on to the Columbia University School of Architecture in 1969 at the height of the Vietnam War protests there, again surrounded by James Gamble Rogers design work.

Rogers joined the architectural firm of Rogers and Butler in 1975, a firm founded by his uncle. In 1979 he left to form his own firm of Butler Rogers Baskett. His early work was not golf-related, but in 1985 he was asked to recommend some improvements to the women's locker room at Shinnecock Hills Golf Club. What he found was an entire clubhouse suffering from longstanding neglect and ad hoc changes. He recommended a complete restoration of the original 1892 Stanford White design. This was accepted, and the renovated clubhouse met with wide attention and acclaim, especially when the club hosted the 1995 US Open.

Since then Rogers's firm has directed thirteen more renovation and restoration projects of historically significant clubhouses, including such masterpieces as the St. Andrews Golf Club (first organized in 1888 and from which came several of Yale's first golf team members), the Sleepy Hollow Country Club (another Stanford White design), Brooklawn Country Club, Wee Burn Country Club (an Addison Mizner design), Wykagyl Country Club, Piping Rock Club (the course designed by C. B. Macdonald and Seth Raynor in 1911) and the Woodway Country Club. The firm is now also designing new clubhouses, including one for the Yale Farms Golf Club, planned by Roland Betts in northwestern Connecticut.

Jim Rogers has remained involved with the Yale Golf Association and served as president from 2003 to 2006. He was especially successful in the Association's fund raising for the restoration of the course. When asked to compare the Yale golf course today with what it was forty years ago, Rogers believes "it seems a lot harder now." He notes that no other course may be as different as Yale's from the regular and long tees.

Theodore "Ted" Weiss
1960 team captain

Seven members of Yale's men's golf team have been chosen for all-American teams, but none has yet made the first team. Only one has been named to the second team, Ted Weiss (Class of 1960), in 1960, the same year that Jack Nicklaus made first team. Weiss went on to a distinguished medical career and still combines his medical practice with ardent recreational golf. Here are some memories he penned in the summer of 2007.

> My knowledge of Yale began in childhood when I listened to a weekly radio program during the 1940s about Frank Merriwell. A fictional Yale man, Merriwell was brave, athletic, and resourceful as he won sports events and thwarted crime. I still remember the theme music from those Saturday mornings. My other introduction to the University was reading about the USGA's holding its 1952 boys junior championship at the Yale course. About that time, golf was becoming important to me, and the chance to attend the college with such a resource was very attractive.

> In 1955 I was one of 128 boys who qualified for the USGA national junior championship at Purdue University in Indiana. I reached the fourth round of the final 16, when I

came to face an opponent who already had quite a reputation as a long hitter, an excellent iron player and was the fortunate possessor of a superior short game. I was worried. Nonetheless, I birdied the ninth hole to turn just one down in the eighteen-hole match. That must have energized my opponent: At ten I hit a driver and 5-iron to the approximately 410 yard par four. He hit driver and wedge for a birdie that beat my par. The final tally was 5 and 4. Maybe you didn't guess, but if I also said he was a blond-headed fellow from Ohio whose initials were JN, you'll know. Having done well in junior golf events in New Orleans and beyond surely helped me to be admitted to Yale in 1956.

Walking onto the golf course's first green that September was an epiphany. It was more of a sculpture than a green. I knew then that I'd come to the right school and that I was going to be educated here in ways I hadn't anticipated. "Heroic" and "epic" came to be among my favorite adjectives for the layout.

Ned Vare was 1957 varsity captain. I don't believe I ever spoke to him, but I was already avid enough about golf history to know that his mother — Glenna Collette Vare — was a golfing legend. Seeing Ned on the team reinforced my impression that an American aristocracy existed at Yale, and I now was observing it up close.

One other aristocrat of golf figured in my memories of that year — Henry Cotton, a former British Open champion. When I got to the course one afternoon, news was that Cotton was playing a round. I hurried out to watch, but by then he'd reached the eighteenth. His shots were struck flawlessly; unfortunately his second — a wood — finished in the rough on the side slope between the upper and lower fairway areas, possibly because he didn't know the best line. Cotton half topped his shot from that difficult lie, and made six. This reinforced for me both how tough the course was, and also how important local knowledge could be.

Number six was my spot on the varsity in my sophomore year. However, the Eastern Intercollegiate Championship played at our course that May was to become the most important competition of my young life. We won the team championship, and I joined the elite sixteen who would compete for the individual title. Very unexpectedly, my first round opponent was the defending champion, Warren Simmons, a national level player from a college in upstate New York. I eventually birdied number eighteen to win 2 up. I continued to play exceptionally well in the afternoon to advance to the semifinals. After winning the next morning's match, I kept up my strong play into the afternoon finals, reaching the 9th tee two-up. But then my wheels came off. I lost 2 up. It was a bitter disappointment after such a run.

For the next two years I played number one. My most important match as a junior came against Princeton at their course. I still remember my nervousness on the final green, facing a downhill four-foot putt to keep myself and the team alive. Happily I made it and went on to win in extra holes, assuring the team's victory. The other salient memory from that year came at the NCAA national championship played at the Eugene (Oregon) Country Club. Parenthetically, I played a practice round with the famous Connecticut amateur, Dick Siderowf, from Duke. He treated us to a hole in one on the 8th with a flawless 7 iron, still vivid in my mind. I advanced though several matches: Simmons, whom I'd beaten the year before in the Easterns, was one I defeated again. I also beat a Walker Cup player from Texas named John Farquhar. Eventually I was in the semifinals, competing against Dick Crawford from the juggernaut University of Houston. He was an excellent player who subsequently turned pro and won on the tour. On the practice tee that morning I had the worst piece of luck in my golfing life. As I was warming up with tee shots, I heard the head/neck of my driver creak. I held it in my hand, and could feel it torque slightly on the shaft as I twisted it. Not knowing what to do, I stuck with the club, trying to turn the head before each drive so that it wouldn't twist unpredictably. I hooked my drive into trouble on the first hole, felt preoccupied throughout the thirty-six-hole match, and lost badly.

Our captain that year was John Suisman from Hartford. Pulling rank, he defeated me at the Easterns after we both had qualified for the individual championship. It was a friendly rivalry though. I stayed with John and his family after college when I played as an amateur in the Insurance City Open on the tour.

For comic relief, let me tell one anecdote about our coach, Al Wilson. Al was more the manager of our team than its coach. He was a funny and unpretentious man who never represented himself as a golf teacher, but rather as the team's organizer and relaxer — which benefited us. His concise advice on the first tee before matches varied, but always elicited a helpful laugh. My favorite was from baseball: "Take two and hit to right."

In my senior year it was flattering to be elected captain. In retrospect this year was anticlimactic. The NCAAs were played at the beautiful Broadmoor course in Colorado, partly designed by Robert Trent Jones, Sr., the father of two of my teammates. Incidentally, Mr. and Mrs. Jones came to several of our home matches. Mrs. Jones was as impressive as her husband. I remember her as perhaps the most gracious and friendly person I've ever met. Having been chosen as a second team All-American — behind such first-teamers as Nicklaus — I participated in a pretournament exhibition match with others on that squad. This was fun, with nothing at stake.

My play in the thirty-six-hole qualifying was mediocre. I missed the playoff for qualifying by two strokes.

In addition to the experiences above, my teammates were another great plus. Classmate Al Gilison was my best friend among these and has remained one since. Bobby Jones (Robert Trent, Jr.) was another close friend. Possessed of almost as classic a swing as that other Bob Jones from the twenties, he was on the varsity each year he was eligible. One of the unique memories with Bobby was playing a round the morning of his wedding in Atlanta. (I was one of the groomsmen.) Phil Lobstein was from Texas and very much in the Hogan mold; happily he was a lot more gregarious. Other teammates I really enjoyed were Ira Thomas, Guy Butterworth, Keith Kittle, Mike Phillips, Frost Walker, and Bill Bayfield. Rees, the other Jones boy, was a freshman when I was a senior, and I knew him only superficially. But by educating these two brothers, what a contribution to American golf Yale made.

A particular pleasure of playing for the varsity was the other wonderful courses we competed on. My favorite was the Taconic Golf Club at Williams College. One year against Harvard we played The Country Club at Brookline. A. W. Tillinghast's Wannamoisett Country Club in Rhode Island for a Brown match was another gem. It also was a treat when a friend, Tony Forstmann — part of my Yale-American aristocracy and a member of the class after mine — took me to play at his Tillinghast-designed club, Winged Foot.

In the year following graduation I gave serious consideration to turning pro. Trying to figure this out, I played as an amateur in several PGA tour tournaments, amateur competitions, and in other open events. Success and frustration followed one another in what felt like about equal measure. Eventually I decided to stop pursuing competitive golf, enrolled in pre-med courses, and went on to become a physician-psychiatrist.

I have returned often to the Yale course over the years, especially to play in the spring association outing and in the Beinecke during early September. In 1994 I won the senior division of the association event with an 81, which included birdies on number four and number eighteen — the only time I can remember doing that. A special pleasure was winning one of the Beinecke net prizes in 2001 with my son, Tony, '02. I also had a chance to give workshops in golf psychology for the women's and men's varsity teams. I enjoyed meeting other university-affiliated golfers at the course during these years, including English professor and college master, Traugott Lawlor; Amy Hueter, the women's golf coach in the nineties and a lawyer; Marge Bell, a member of the women's varsity; Dick Granger, the late pediatrician; and my former teammate, Giles Payne, whom I came to know much better.

My most recent visit to the course came at my 45th reunion in 2005 when I just took a nostalgic ride around without playing. Thinking of the beauty there reminds me of another important person in my Yale memories, Harry Meusel, the longtime superintendent. In his loving attention to the course was more than a little of the poet. The Japanese garden Harry put in near the pond at number thirteen is a charming example. When he retired in the 1990s, I realized how important, if nearly subliminal, his contribution to my pleasure had been over the decades.

The other noteworthy person in my years after Yale has been the longtime varsity coach, David Paterson. It's hard to encompass all of Dave's virtues. Most succinctly, he is the complete Scottish golfer, friendly, funny, astute, articulate, and supportive of students. He is able to be either intense or relaxed. And finally, he is possessed of a wonderful golf game.

He's been a great friend and a great enhancement to the university's golf scene.

By now I've been a doctor for over forty years. I'm happy with this choice — for me a better one than a career in golf. But, recounting these stories about my Yale golf experience makes me realize that, while medicine has filled my head, golf has filled my heart.

Varsity Golf Team, 1960. Front, L–R: Henry Lobstein, Tom Triplett; back, L–R: Coach Al Wilson, Robert T. Jones, Jr., Al Gilison, Captain Ted Weiss, Mike Phillips, Frosty Walker, Manager Huntley Davenport

Robert "Bobby" Trent Jones, Jr.
Varsity golfer and course designer

Bobby Jones (Class of 1961) has designed more than 200 golf courses in thirty-eight countries on six continents. As he has acknowledged, he could not have accomplished this without "a creative father and a wise mother." His connections to golf and to Yale go back even further. His paternal grandfather was attending grade school in Rochester, New York, where he enjoyed pulling the pigtails of the girl sitting in front of him. One day she turned around and told him, "If you'll stop, I'll give you a dime so you can take the trolley to the end of the line, then walk a mile to the golf club where my uncle will give you a job as a caddie." That he did, and there he learned the game from the club pro who was none other than Walter Hagen. Jones later taught the game to his own son, Robert Trent Jones, Sr., who was determined to become a golf course architect. As an undergraduate at Cornell, he created his own course of study, combining agriculture and liberal arts. Both his maternal grandfather and great grandfather were Yale graduates. Great grandfather Rees grew up in Cincinnati, where his athletic ability came to the attention of Horace Taft (brother of William Howard Taft, both Yale graduates). Taft arranged for him to attend the Taft School and later Yale on scholarships linked to his football playing. He played for Coach Walter Camp and, after graduating in 1896, participated in the first modern Olympic Games as a sprinter. Jones paid for his Atlantic passage by shoveling coal on a Grace Line ship.

Jones learned to play golf from the club pro and from his father. In the 1950s they were both good players. Bob was a finalist in the 1956 Metropolitan Junior Championship, and he and his father finished third in the 1957 New Jersey Father-Son Championship. Bob was a member of the 1956 US Junior team that played the U.K. team at Winged Foot. Based on his performance there, especially on the famous tenth hole, Tommy Armour offered to instruct him in course management.

When it came time to decide on a college, his father favored Princeton and his mother preferred Yale. While still in high school, Jones had played the "interesting and unique" Yale golf course, and that made his decision easy. At Yale he was "frightened" by the difficulty of the academic work, but he "worked hard" and did well. He learned how to study and be curious, especially in regard to "cultural history." The only course that directly related to his profession was geology.

Making the golf team was not easy because Jones was competing against five former state junior champions. But, he made the team by winning the last three holes of his match in a March snowstorm. The team won the EIGA Championship twice and went to the NCAA nationals in Oregon and Colorado. Jones enjoyed the "psychological" challenge of match play. His parents were very supportive; his mother Iona attended every home match, and his father came when he was not traveling. Coach Wilson's son Al caddied for Jones and often borrowed his 1958 blue Impala convertible for an evening date, while Jones was having a post-match dinner with his mother.

After he graduated from Yale, Jones attended Stanford Law School, again at the urging of his mother. She thought that he should train for a "substantial job" and not follow his father into the "cottage industry of golf design." This time, his father won. He joined his father's business in 1962, at the time when Robert Trent Jones, Sr., was transforming golf architecture. Bob concentrated on designing and building courses on the West Coast and internationally. His father taught him the merits and demerits of design by Macdonald, Banks, Tillinghast, Ross, and his favorite, Mackenzie, as well as his own. His father had first taught him how to strike a golf ball, now he taught him how to design and build a course. He had another teacher as well, Tommy Armour. When Armour taught Jones course management, he pointed out that in Scotland the "features" of the courses had names like Redan, Hell's Bunker, etc. These features dictated club selection and how you "worked the ball." Armour, without meaning to, had also been teaching course design.

In 1973, Jones formed his own company, Robert Trent Jones II Golf Course Architects, in Palo Alto, California. He served as president of the American Society of Golf Course Architects and in 1993, published the book *Golf by Design*. It is a clever title because the book is about course design, but it also a primer on how a golfer should manage his or her game by attending closely to the designed "features" of tee, fairway, bunker and green, to the illusions that these features can create, and to natural elements of wind and rain. The foreword to the book was written by five-time Open champion Tom Watson, who, along with former USGA president Sandy Tatum, assisted Jones in designing of one of his most acclaimed courses in the United States, The Links at Spanish Bay in Pebble Beach, California. Other notable designs among his now more than 200 are the Prince Course at Princeville on Kauai, rated sixty-third in the United States by *Golf Digest*; Moscow Country Club, the first course built in Russia; Spring City Golf & Lake Resort, ranked number one in China; Le Prince de Provence, ranked number one in France; and Miklagard Golf Club, ranked number one in Norway.

Jones believes strongly that his Yale education made him appreciate cultural history, which helped him considerably in facing the challenges of working around the world. But wherever the location, he looks on his work as "stage craft, [as] setting up the game and creating a challenge" for the player. He doesn't believe technology has diminished the value of older courses like Merion. To him a "golf course is alive" and, like Augusta National, often "a work in progress." He takes great pride in having worked in the "golden age" of course design.

Rees Jones
Golf course architect and "The Open Doctor II"

The final round of the US Open is traditionally played on Father's Day. In 1951 at Oakland Hills Country Club, when Ben Hogan was presented with the winner's trophy, he said, "I'm glad I brought this course, this monster, to its knees." Neither he, nor anyone else, had broken par until the final round. That was the first time that the USGA had a course redesigned for the championship. It was the work of Robert Trent Jones, Sr., who would do this so often that he would become known as "The Open Doctor." In 1954, at age thirteen, his younger son, Rees, was given the job of measuring drives on the fairways at Baltusrol Golf Club, so that his father could analyze and plan the relocation and positioning of bunkers in preparation for future US Open sites.

Rees Jones (Class of 1963) was born not far from Baltusrol, in Montclair, New Jersey. After attending Montclair High School and working summers on his father's course construction crew, he chose Yale for his college education. This was quite natural, since his mother's father, grandfather, and other relatives had attended Yale. She believed he should have a liberal education before he chose a profession. Jones says that Yale was "a great choice" for him, since the education "expanded his life" and there he made many lifelong friends. Even though growing up with his famous father, he had been exposed to all the aspects of golf course design, it wasn't until his junior year that Jones decided to practice that "craft." After graduation he studied the technical aspects of his chosen profession, such as drafting and landscape design at Harvard.

With both a liberal and technical education and the "learning done in the field," he "had the best of all worlds."

At Yale, Jones failed by one stoke to qualify for the freshman golf team,. But, because his older brother Bobby had been on the team, he knew Coach Al Wilson, who asked him to be the manager of the freshman team. In retrospect, Jones thinks that he was probably chosen because he had a car and could help transport the team to away matches. As a junior, he became manager of the varsity and, for two years, practiced with the team. In his junior year, he "was playing well in practice," and the team qualified for the NCAA national championship. Coach Wilson picked him for the team that traveled to the tournament that was played at the Duke University course designed by his father in 1957. Several decades later, one of his daughters attended Duke. In 1994 he redesigned the course, making it "stronger and longer and with recontoured greens." He is very proud of this work, which allowed Duke to host the NCAA championship again in 2001.

Like Rees, his father was an admirer of the work of C. B. Macdonald, especially his work at the National Golf Links of America and Yale. His father came to watch matches at Yale during the years that Jones's brother and he were there but never played the course. As with most Macdonald/Raynor projects, Rees believes that Seth Raynor "did most of the work at Yale." Raynor "was like my father's design associate, Roger Rulewich." As far as design is concerned, Jones now considers Macdonald, Raynor, and Charles Banks all together. He was first exposed to their work at Yale and since then as a member of National Golf Links of America (Macdonald) and the Montclair Golf Club (Banks) as well as through his work of redesign and restoration at Monterey Peninsula Country Club (Raynor) and Hackensack Golf Club in New Jersey (Banks).

Jones joined his father's firm in 1965 and then started his own company, Rees Jones, Inc. in Montclair in 1974. In 1978 he became the youngest president of the American Society of Golf Course Architects. *Golf Digest* named him Architect of the Year in 1995. The Golf Course Superintendents Association of American awarded him the Old Tom Morris Award in 2004. The award had gone to his father in 1987. The unofficial title of Open Doctor passed to the son when Rees redesigned The Country Club for the 1988 US Open.

Rees Jones, Inc.

Rees Jones, 2004

Rees Jones now has more than 140 golf courses to his credit. Though most of them are original designs, he is best known for his redesign work. These courses have been the sites for seven US Opens, six PGA Championships, three Ryder Cup competitions, two Walker Cups, and one President's Cup. He redesigned East Lake Golf Club in Atlanta (Bobby Jones's home course) for the PGA Tour Championship. In addition to the redesign of his father's original design of the Duke University course, Jones redesigned Baltusrol Golf Club, Congressional Country Club, and Hazeltine National Golf Club for US Opens twenty or more years after his father had done the same. The other Open redesigned courses are The Country Club, Pinehurst No. 2, the Black Course at Bethpage State Park, and Torrey Pines South. Three original designs are on the *Golf Digest* 100-best-course list (Ocean Forest Golf Club, Atlantic Golf Club, and The Golf Club at Briar's Creek).

In addition to his brother, Jones has known others who have been part of the Yale golf story. He knew Jess Sweetser very well, meeting him first when Sweetser visited their home as a frequent guest of his father (who "greatly admired" Sweetser's golfing triumphs as a player and Walker Cup captain). "Jess was a great influence on my father and took a liking to his sons." Later Jones met him many times at Yale reunions. Jones was well acquainted with Mark McCormack, whom he considered "the first to see golf as a business as well as a game," beginning with his television marketing of the Big Three (Palmer, Nicklaus, and Player). He went on to "elevate the economics of golf" and many other sports. Jones knew Charles Fraser even better through their service on the board of the Urban Land Institute.

When asked his opinion about a "standard ball" to combat the effective shortening of courses by new equipment, Jones responded that "all equipment improvements are positive for the average golfer. A 'standard ball' is a good idea for the professionals, but it will not be adopted because of the loss of revenue to manufacturers and the experience of the 'square groove' litigation."

Reflecting on his undergraduate days at the Yale Golf Course, Jones said that "he was lucky to be introduced to a great golf course over four years and to learn that a course doesn't have to be perfect, but that bad bounces and blind holes make it a course that you never tire of playing." He gets ideas for designing from playing old courses, as Macdonald did before him and Old and Young Tom Morris did before C. B. After his recent tour of the course, Jones said that "Yale is still one of the great courses in America. Length is not as important as the angles and hazards, which dictate the shots that make it, like Pinehurst No. 2, a stout test of golf, which has stood the test of time." Therefore, the "Open Doctor" will not be needed at the Yale Golf Course. As he himself opined, the course as it is now would be an excellent site for the women's and men's Amateur or the women's Open championships. "That is a credit to Macdonald and Raynor eighty years ago and to the University today."

Roger G. Rulewich
Golf course architect

Roger Rulewich (Class of 1958) arrived at Yale as a scholarship student and non-golfer. By the time he graduated, with a civil engineering degree, he had become "hooked on the game." During those four years he had often gone to the "beautiful course" on his bicycle to play for the $1.00 greens fee or just to walk in his "retreat."

Upon graduating Rulewich went to work for a large engineering and landscape design firm in New York City. After three years he decided to pursue his interest in architecture and submitted his resume to the alumni placement service. It arranged an interview with an architect who turned out to be Robert Trent Jones, Sr. Rulewich was surprised to learn that Jones designed golf courses, not buildings, but he took the position Jones offered him. One of his first assignments was to design and build several bridges at Laurence Rockefeller's golf course in Woodstock, Vermont.

Over the next thirty-four years, Rulewich became an architect who, as Ron Whitten wrote, "produced stunning courses in the exact (and exacting) style of Robert Trent Jones." From 1931 to 2000 more than 500 courses in forty states and thirty-five countries were attributed to Jones. Rulewich became his chief designer and in the 1980s and 1990s, became the "poster boy of unsung golf course architects." Whitten wrote that in 2004, he watched Yale graduate, Heather Daly-Donofrio, win

the LPGA Tournament of Champions, held at his favorite course on Alabama's Robert Trent Jones Trail, in Mobile — the Crossing course at Magnolia Grove Golf Club, actually designed by Roger Rulewich.

From 1989 to 1992, Roger Rulewich designed and managed the largest golf construction project in US history. Dr. David Bronner, CEO of the Retirement System of Alabama, devised a plan to diversify the assets of the state pension fund and bring tourist dollars into the state by building seven, new, multi-course golf facilities (324 holes) — the RTJ Golf Trail. Very few know what Rulewich did for this project, and he says he "could care less. The people that need to know that I was heavily involved with the Trail know,

Roger Rulewich, 2000

and that is what is important. Those people are potential clients and my peers." Jones was age eighty-six when it was completed and essentially served as a sounding board for Rulewich's work. The Jones firm closed its offices in 1995, and Rulewich and a select group from the office formed The Roger Rulewich Group.

On the recommendation of David Paterson, the University hired Rulewich to renovate and restore all of the bunkers of the course. Using old construction photographs, aerial photographs, site reviews, and other documents, every existing bunker was returned to its original condition and properly drained. The leftside bunker on the first fairway was reshaped to bring it into play. Those greenside bunkers at the second, twelfth, thirteenth, sixteenth, and seventeenth holes that had been removed were restored with drainage. Only the hillside bunkers on the tenth and eighteenth fairways were not restored.

As Rulewich has noted, the only bunker work that remains is around the third green, the pond-side right half of which was eliminated in the 1940s. He has expressed the hope that the green itself can be restored to its original size and shape and that the bunkering can then be brought closer to the original.

Yale Athletics Archives

Tenth tee in left foreground, circa 1930. The drive had to carry the two bunkers, which have not been restored. The second shot on the 18th hole had to carry the large bunker located at the top of the hill in the far upper right, also not restored.

Herbert V. Kohler, Jr.
Innovative golf resort developer

Herb Kohler's (Class of 1965) route to his Yale graduation in 1965 was unusual. His mother died when he was thirteen. He recalls being such a handful for his father that he was sent off to prep school. After one year at Exeter, he was asked to leave. He did finally graduate from Choate in 1957 and, like his father, went on to Yale. He left Yale after one year. The dean, after assessing Kohler's freshman performance, challenged him "to find a purpose in life." He moved to Switzerland and studied advanced math and physics (in German), he recalls proudly. Next he attended Knox College in Illinois and studied theater, before returning to Yale. He graduated with a B.S. in industrial administration. Kohler took a corporate job, but shortly his father asked him to join the family business. Two years later, in 1972, his father died unexpectedly and Kohler took control of the company.

Herb Kohler is now chairman of the board and president of the company his grandfather founded in Kohler, Wisconsin.

The Kohler Company is a world leader in products for the kitchen and bath. The Kohler Interiors Group is a leading manufacturer of power systems and furniture. In the last twenty-five years, Kohler developed a fourth major business in hospitality and real estate. "Destination Kohler" and "Destination St. Andrews" have become just that for serious golfers.

Herb Kohler first used 1,000 acres along seven miles of the Sheboygan River to develop River Wildlife, a private hunting and fishing club. To accommodate guests, he converted a former dormitory for the company's immigrant factory workers into the American Club. Then he built four golf courses for his guests. Pete Dye designed two courses at Blackwolf Run and two at Whistling Straits. The Straits course at Whistling Straits was the site of the 2004 PGA Championship. Kohler, Wisconsin is going to be a destination for major championships and events for some time to come, with commitments for the 2007 US Senior Open, 2010 PGA Championship, 2012 US Women's Open, 2015 PGA, and the 2020 Ryder Cup.

Kohler Co.

Herbert V. Kohler, Jr., 2005

The Kohler Company's latest acquisitions are the Old Course Hotel and the Duke's course, resort, and spa at St Andrews, Scotland. The Duke's course was designed ten years ago by Peter Thomson, but it has been redesigned and renovated by Tom Liddy, who apprenticed with Pete Dye. It certainly appears that the name Herb Kohler deserved to appear on the cover of the January 2005 Golf Digest, as one of the "top five golf people of the year."

Charles E. Fraser
Course developer and conservationist

The father of Charles Fraser (Yale Law School Class of 1953) was in the timber business, and, in 1949, he bought 5,000 acres on the southern tip of the forty-one square-mile Hilton Head Island, South Carolina for logging. Son Charlie Fraser worked in the island logging camp during the summer of 1950, after he graduated from the University of Georgia and before he entered Yale Law School. At the time there were only about 500 people living on Hilton Head. They were mostly farmers and oyster workers who traveled by boat to Savannah to sell their products. Fraser was entranced by the island and saw its potential to attract many more people to its beautiful beaches, virgin pine forests and rich groves of great live oaks. He convinced his father to give him a twenty-year note on the land and complete legal control. Fraser entered law school in the fall and made the development of a master plan the focus of his education.

"I started talking to my Yale professors about land-use covenants, tax law, and other things about Hilton Head Island and got a graduate student at Yale Architectural School to do his master's thesis on the south end of Hilton Head," said Fraser, who earned his law degree in 1953. *"I spent six years researching every conceivable source on resort development."* It was all information he would need to convince investors, banks and various other skeptics that the project could work. *"I was probably told 50 times between 1954 and 1956 that the era of beach resorts was over. The belief was that, with improved highways, all the important families of Savannah and Charleston — who considered themselves the only market that mattered for these beach places — were going to the mountains for the summer."*

Two other challenges that could have kept people away were heat and mosquitoes. But timing and the time he spent researching eventually paid off. The first bridge connecting Hilton Head to the mainland was built in 1956, a year before construction began at Sea Pines Plantation. Fraser found ways to battle Hilton Head's summer elements. He employed a then-revolutionary process to fight mosquito and other insect infestation, using a light aerosol spray along the marsh's edge during the full moon. And he made Sea Pines the South's first totally air-conditioned resort.

Fraser's plan was to develop the island for the enjoyment of the new resort residents without destroying the local environment and its natural beauty. He mandated that the large populations of herons, egrets, otter and deer were not to be harmed by Sea Pines' development and that the fewest possible number of trees were to be removed during construction. To complement rather than overpower the surroundings, he also wrote into community bylaws that homes had to be approved by an architectural review board and use only muted colors and lighting schemes. No home could exceed three stories, and no tree wider than six inches in diameter could be cut in the entire community. The homes and streets were designed around the trees. He was among the first to use the covenants and deed restrictions that he had studied at Yale Law School to protect the environment.

In 1959 the first of two courses was built in Sea Pines. A third course was completed in 1969, just in time for the Sea Pines Heritage Golf Classic at Harbour Town Golf Links. By then, the year-round population had grown to 2,500. Arnold Palmer won that first Heritage, and enthusiastic galleries and television audiences inspired a growth in tourists and permanent residents that continues to this day.

Interestingly, Charlie Fraser never played golf, and he knew nothing about the game, but he understood trends and tastes and was a great salesman. By hiring Jack Nicklaus and Pete Dye to design Harbour Town, he was able to attract a PGA tournament. The free publicity it generated for the growing number of golfers of the 1960s and 1970s was a salesman's dream. As proof of how little Fraser really knew about golf, Pete Dye likes to tell about what he saw Charlie doing on the first day of the tournament in 1969. "We really didn't have the course ready. I was still putting sand in the bunker on the 18th hole when the first group on Thursday was coming up the 14th. A PGA official came running up to me and wanted to know, who that guy was that was going around the course removing all the red, yellow, and white stakes. Of course it was Charlie, who thought they were construction stakes and had to be removed when the job was done."

Charles Fraser sold Sea Pines Plantation in 1983, but he continued to live on the island. He remained active in other developments and in consulting. He received many community-planning awards, including the Urban Land Institute Heritage Award, which had been given out only five times in seventy-five years. He died in a boating accident in 2002.

Mark McCormack
Pioneer sports agent

In 1954 the Law School graduated another individual who, like Charles Fraser, was to make a significant mark in the world of golf. Mark McCormack (Yale Law School Class of 1954) was voted the "Most Powerful Man in Tennis" by *Tennis Magazine* and the "Most Powerful Man in Golf" by *Golf Digest*. In 1990, *Sports Illustrated* called him "The Most Powerful Man in Sport." When he was inducted in the World Golf Hall of Fame in 2006, McCormack was called "the man who invented modern golf ... and who reshaped all of sports." Here's how this came about.

McCormack was born in western Pennsylvania and went to the College of William & Mary. He played on the college golf team and was good enough to qualify for the 1958 US Open at Southern Hills. To keep his game in tune, one would assume that he played the Yale Golf Course while he attended the law school. After graduation he joined a prestigious law firm in Cleveland. However, his entrepreneurial skill and energy led him within two years to start a company, National Sports Marketing, that booked golf exhibitions for some of the leading pros of that era.

Arnold Palmer was also from western Pennsylvania. They first met in 1950 when the Wake Forest University golf team played against William & Mary. In 1956, McCormack was in the US Army, stationed at Camp Gordon in Augusta Georgia. He attended the Masters and delivered a putter to Palmer, from their mutual friend, Bob Toski. McCormack first broached the subject of National Sports Marketing representing Palmer at the 1959 Carling Open, a PGA tournament in Cleveland. Several months later Palmer told McCormack that he wanted someone to do more than book Monday golf exhibitions. Palmer wanted "one man" to handle all his business affairs "exclusively." Palmer's model for this person was Clifford Roberts, who managed the affairs of the Augusta National Golf Club and of President Eisenhower. Even though McCormack had to give up National Sports Management, he agreed to become Palmer's agent and manager. The deal was done with a simple handshake. Not long thereafter, with Palmer's blessing, McCormack signed a talented South African newcomer, Gary Player, and a young American professional, Jack Nicklaus. Either inadvertently or with incredible foresight, McCormack had signed the "Big Three" who would dominate golf for decades and promote the sport's global appeal. For this endeavor, he founded a new company, the International Management Group, known by its initials, IMG.

McCormack increased his first three client's endorsement value by creating a made-for-TV event, 'Big Three Golf', which served as a marketing tool for both the game and his star players. With an eye for the best talent, McCormack was constantly expanding his company. The first tennis player he signed was Rod Laver; his first hockey player was Gordie Howe, and his first skier was Jean-Claude Killy! He also grasped the concept of vertical integration. Outside the United States there are some tournaments where IMG has designed the golf course, built it, and managed it. Then it managed the tournament and, through its TV arm, Trans World International (TWI), televised the event in which most of the competitors were IMG clients. When McCormack created the World Golf Ranking in the mid 1980s, it was derisively dismissed by some as an attempt by IMG to get more attention — and more money — to its non-American players, like Norman and Faldo. That was true, but it is also true that those players deserved more attention, and the World Ranking is now used by every major championship in determining its field.

The company has also grown to be a major player in the football market as well as representing athletes from rugby, cricket, motor racing, and a host of other sports. IMG's TWI is the world's largest independent television sports production company and rights distributor. The group also owns and represents many major sporting events around the world, operates several sports academies, and runs agencies for classical music artists and fashion models.

Golf, however, remained McCormack's game. In 1996 he showed again that he hadn't lost his touch when IMG became the agent for new pro, Tiger Woods. In the next decade, Tiger won sixty-six tournaments including twelve major championships. McCormack's first task for Palmer in 1959 had been to try to renegotiate his $5,000-a-year contract with the Wilson Sporting Goods Company. He failed at that, and Palmer was not able to start the Arnold Palmer Golf Company until the Wilson contract expired in 1963. IMG's first task for Woods was to negotiate his initial Nike contract for $50,000,000. Palmer became the first golfing millionaire; Tiger is on his way to becoming the first sports billionaire. Maybe *Sports Illustrated* had it right — Mark McCormack was "The Most Powerful Man in Sports."

Philip F. Nelson
Player, professor, and Golf Committee chairman

The 1970s were not good times for Yale golf. The head professional and varsity coach, Al Wilson, left in 1970. An assistant football coach, Paul Amodio, was also the golf coach from 1970 to 1974, and Paul Lufkin had the job for 1974. The team won no league championships during that period. Superintendent Harry Meusel maintained the course under the direction of Widdy Neale, the Athletics Department business manager. The Eli Club, a club within a club, held tournaments for nonstudent members of the course, but very few students were using the course for golf (although some reportedly did come out for late-night, back-to-nature pursuits!). University officials considered out-sourcing the course management, and there was even talk of selling the golf course. Yale Corporation members Erwin Miller and Bill Beinecke vetoed that radical move, but there was widespread concern about the course's future.

Yale University president Kingman Brewster decided not to turn management over to an outside company but rather to upgrade the golf program from within. It surprised some that he turned to a music professor to begin the effort. However, Philip Nelson had come to Yale in 1970 as the dean of the Graduate School of Music, but he also brought a 5-handicap. Nelson was born in Minnesota and began playing golf at age seven. After graduating from the University of North

Carolina at Chapel Hill, he played well enough in the early 1950s to compete as an amateur in several PGA events before turning to the scholarly world of music history, receiving his Ph.D. in 1958 from the same school.

President Brewster appointed Dean Nelson to chair a committee charged with finding someone to fill the new position of Director of Golf. The other committee members were Dick Tettlebach, Burt Resnik, Herb Emanuelson, Richard Broadbent, and Herb Wind. Professor Nelson remembers that they did in fact find the golf program "in disarray, with Widdy running the course as his own." For the Director of Golf they considered many prominent people; several were suggested by Byron Nelson, who was a friend of (though no relation to) Philip Nelson. But, the name David Paterson kept coming up. His lifelong background in golf, his apprenticeship in course and club management at Turnberry and subsequent professional directorships in Bermuda and the Northeast, his playing experience in British and US PGA tournaments, and his education in both science and art, perfectly matched the committee's desire for a "golf person, but one with an intellectual and cultural background." Phil Nelson remains very proud of his role in selecting and bringing to Yale, David Paterson, who ushered in a new era of Yale golf by upgrading the golf program, developing winning traditions in both men's and women's golf, and working towards the restoration of the course and its facilities.

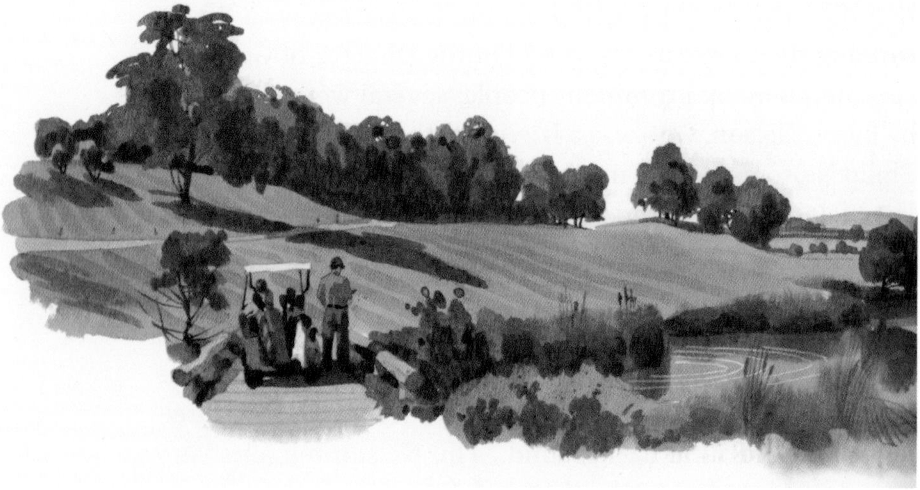

1975–2000
The David Paterson Era

David Paterson
Director of Golf and men's and women's team coach

When Dave Paterson retired in 2008, the "Scottish Bulldog," as he has affectionately come to be known, was one of the longest-serving coaches in NCAA golf history. In thirty-three years as Yale's golf coach he led the men's team to eight Ivy League titles and twelve individual titles and to five New England Division 1 championships and nine individual titles. Two of his teams played in the NCAA National Golf Championship and ten of his teams qualified for the NCAA Regional Tournament. Five of his players have ventured into professional golf. Peter Teravainen (1978) and Bob Heintz (1992) established long, impressive careers, winning a number of major events. Two other past Ivy League Champions played professionally for a few years: Ken Rizvi (1997) on the Gateway Tour and Chris Eckerle (2002) on the Hooters Tour. Paterson began the women's varsity team and, as its coach, worked closely with Heather Daly-Donofrio (1991), who went on to a career as an LPGA pro.

Despite this distinguished coaching record, Paterson himself is the first to insist that he is much prouder of his team members' successes in life than on the course. Certainly the testimonies of former players, from his first team in 1975 to his final team in 2008, speak of the lasting influence of his teachings. Equally important, as Director of Golf for almost as many years, Paterson was the key individual who finally

David Paterson, circa 1980

brought professional management to all aspects of the golf course and the golf program.

David Paterson was born and raised on golf courses in Scotland. His father was a golf professional and Head Green Keeper at the Fereneze Golf Club and later at the Paisley Golf Club, both the suburbs of Glasgow where Paterson spent most of his youth. He was one of six children, including three brothers who played golf together endlessly during the long summer evenings. "We only knew golf and sheep," as Paterson put it in an interview (the sheep handling came from the British government mandate during World War II that sheep graze on golf courses for maintenance). He grew up helping his father with whatever tasks were needed, including collecting sheep droppings off the course. Picking up the game himself, with few formal lessons and plenty of practice, he was already playing to a four-handicap at age twelve.

After three years of mandatory service in the Royal Air Force, Paterson started studying chemistry at the Paisley Polytechnic College near Glasgow with a view to a medical laboratory career. But, one day while running an errand for his father, he came across Ian Marchbank, who had just joined the world-famous Turnberry Resort Hotel and Golf Club as the head professional. Knowing the young man's reputation as a golfer, Marchbank offered him a job as his assistant on the spot, and the very next day Paterson was a golf pro. He remained at Turnberry for four years in the late 1950s, working six-day weeks, often from 8 A.M. to 11 P.M. Turnberry was a five-star resort. Paterson picked up all aspects of golf management and become a respected teacher of the game. He also had the chance to meet and play with a wide range of political dignitaries and business leaders, including then-President Dwight Eisenhower. Ike drove over in an open, white, Rolls-Royce convertible from an apartment at the nearby Culzean Castle that he had maintained since his days as World War II Supreme Allied Commander in Europe

Paterson became intrigued with the United States by listening every Saturday morning in his home to the popular radio program, "Letters from America," which was produced and narrated by the famed journalist, Alistair Cooke. In his fourth year at Turnberry, he jumped at an opportunity to become head pro at the Riddle's Bay Golf and Country Club in Bermuda. As a member of the British PGA, he was allowed to play seven US PGA events each year. During the summer off-season in Bermuda, he qualified for such tournaments as the Western Open, the Cleveland Open, and the Canadian Open. Although his winnings were modest, it was a wonderful experience for Paterson, and the many friends he made helped him make a permanent move to the United States.

In 1964, Paterson was invited up to be the assistant pro at Brooklawn Country Club, in Bridgeport, Connecticut, where he worked for four years before becoming head pro at the Country Club of Fairfield. Five years later, he saw an advertisement in the *Bridgeport Post* newspaper for an opening at Yale as Director of Golf. He was offered the position and accepted it on the condition that he could also coach the golf team. Paterson claims it was the wisest move he ever made because, without a close connection to the students, the job would be less personal and much removed from campus life. The University accepted his condition.

It was a critical moment for golf at Yale. Distracted by campus turmoil and disinterested in the course, the University administration had seriously considered selling the entire Tomkins property to a housing developer. It was only the strenuous dissent by trustees, such as William Beinecke, and a few faculty, such as Philip Nelson, then Dean of the School of Music and an avid golfer, that thwarted what would have been the demise of golf at Yale. As profiled earlier, Nelson headed the search committee that hired Paterson.

Though the course was safe from developers' bulldozers, Yale golf still lacked coordinated management when Paterson arrived. Joe Vancisin, the men's basketball coach, was assigned to run the golf team, and Gene Sheehan operated the small pro shop. Harry Meusel, always with inadequate staff, was superintendent of the course, and Widdy Neale controlled the business side of the course from his Connecticut Golf Association office on Howe Street. Paterson noted that it took him nine months to get a look at the books! Once in his hands, he raised prices. The student daily fee was doubled to $2.00 and the annual staff membership raised to $75. Course rules were tightened, practice on the course was prohibited, and a ball rental system installed on the driving range, all moves strongly opposed by the existing membership.

Paterson began immediately to build programs, draw attention to the course, and improve the course. He created the William S. Beinecke Annual Member-Guest Tournament, which remains a centerpiece on the annual calendar, and the Widdy Neale Invitational, a popular state-wide event that sadly was discontinued. He successfully pursued funding for a new irrigation system, a new putting green, a chipping green, and an expansion of the driving range. And, finally, the Beinecke family's Prospect Hill Foundation funded a new clubhouse that was completed in 1984. Under Paterson's guidance the first ungendered club tournament organization was created, so that men and women competed equally in all club events. The term "ladies tees" was eliminated from the scorecard; they were renamed the "forward tees."

In the course of his career as Director of Golf, Paterson attracted a long list of state and national golf events to the Yale Course, including two Connecticut Opens, two Connecticut Amateur Championships, the 1980 National

Insurance Youth Classic, the 1988 USGA National Junior Championship, and the 1990 Ben Hogan New Haven Open. Nike (now Nationwide) tour events in 1991 and 1992 brought celebrity pros, such as John Daly, Stewart Cink, Jeff Maggert, and Tom Lehman to Yale, and, in 1995, Paterson arranged for Yale to host the first World Special Olympics Golf Championship. With a small field of famous Senior PGA stars, he started the Yale Golf Classic, which has become a major support for Yale athletics.

At first Paterson found the atmosphere on the golf team to be rather casual; long hair was in, uniforms absent, and practice was a few holes after class. He did inherit quality players such as three-time, All-American Peter Teravainen '78, and he started recruiting immediately. Other All-Americans followed, such as Thomas (Trip) Long '80 and Bill Huddleston '85. In recent years, Paterson proudly added Academic All-Americans Bob Heintz '92, Ken Rizvi '97, Louis Aurilio '01, Eddie Brockner '01, Chris Eckerle '02 (twice), Adam Cyrus '02, Ben Levy '04 and Mark Matza '07 (twice).

With perhaps unrealistic ambition to add another national title to Yale's record twenty-one championships, Paterson strengthened and expanded the men's tournament schedule by traveling the country to play the strongest teams, fueled by his belief that performance can only be improved by competing against the very best golfers. In an effort to attract top college golfers, he created the Yale Fall Intercollegiate Tournament (subsequently named the Macdonald Cup) and later, the Yale Spring Opener, which inaugurates New England's college golf season. To elevate New England college golf and bring the Yale course to the attention of the NCAA, Paterson hosted the 1991 and 1995 NCAA Regional Championships and several New England NCAA Division I Championships.

Coach Paterson saw that Yale's two-week spring term recess offered special opportunity to enhance the golf team experience. In 1980, he took the team on the first two-week tour of the United Kingdom, where they played a series of matches against leading British universities, including Oxford, Cambridge, Glasgow, Edinburgh, and St. Andrews. He also arranged matches against many famous Royal golf clubs, among them Blackheath, St. George's, Cinque Ports, Liverpool, Troon, and the Honourable Company of Edinburgh Golfers at Muirfield. Every four years since 1980, the UK trip is a highlight of the program that offers each team member a memorable cultural and athletic experience.

David Paterson, "The Scottish Bulldog," in 2008

Paterson has also played an important role in promoting New England college golf and raising its stature within the NCAA. He served three terms as chairman of the New England District NCAA Selection Committee for the NCAA Regional Tournament. When the NCAA's golf committee proposed to eliminate district selections in favor of selection by national rankings, Paterson led the effort to retain district selection. He managed to stall the change, although alas, for only two years. Paterson earned NCAA New England District Coach-of-the-Year award four times, and he has been honored by the Golf Coaches Association of America with its 25-year and its 30-year Distinguished Service Awards.

Paterson served four terms as president of the Ivy League Coaches Association, and he helped move the Ivy Championship from a schedule that rotated the championship through the four Ivy school courses to a neutral venue. The tournament is held in April, so snow was often still on the ground at the Cornell and Dartmouth courses. The first neutral site was Bethpage State Park, the Black course, where the Ivy Championship was held for eleven years.

Paterson took the women's program from its infancy to a competitive team within New England. Shortly after the team's first victory at the Mount Holyoke Invitational, he handed over the program to its first full-time coach, Darci Wilson.

The Ivy League restricts varsity golf competition to twenty days a year. The New England climate that shortens the fall and spring golf seasons and the stiff academic requirements of Yale College were conditions that the Scottish Bulldog accepted with equanimity. He was the rare college coach who demanded of his players and expected their total commitment to the game, but who also appreciated, indeed, insisted, that they came to Yale for its academic excellence. Paterson has been a nationally recognized golf instructor and was always ready with an astute appraisal and well-chosen word of advice, but he treated all of his players with respect and avoided over-coaching them.

During events at Yale, especially the Spring Opener, Paterson took a measure of pride in offering the challenges of the course in the often harsh conditions of Connecticut's freezing northeasterlies in April. Snow was regarded as casual water and not a cause for cancellation. Golf is never easy, and Paterson's philosophy of keeping a steady focus, playing within one's abilities, and always grinding it out has served his legions of players in their careers as well as in their games.

One of Paterson's longstanding commitments was to develop ways to attract alumni back to play the course and remain supportive of Yale golf. He developed the annual Beinecke tournament and other events to encourage this, and his tours of Scottish, English, and Irish golf courses — for the golf teams every four years, but also for alumni and course members — are legendary.

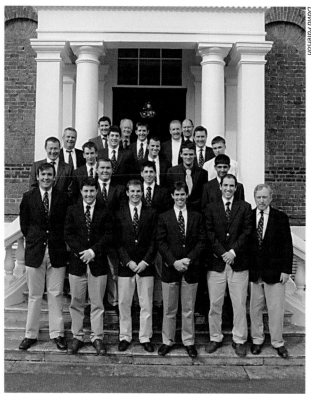

David Paterson

The Yale Men's Golf Team at Blackheath, spring term recess, 2008

In 2008, Dave Paterson finally retired as coach of the men's team, although he can still be found many days at the course, giving lessons, offering advice, and telling stories in his distinctive brogue. His latest legacy is the David Paterson Golf Technology Center, a state-of-the-art training facility in the Payne Whitney Gymnasium. With a course simulator, camera, and launch monitor, it gives the teams opportunities for year-round practice. He bequeathed to Peter Pulaski, who succeeded him as Director of Golf in 2000 and who shares his passion for teaching, a plan for an outdoor practice facility at the course that is now becoming a reality. He has turned over the men's golf team to one of his own former players, Colin

Sheehan (Class of 1997), who worked as assistant coach of the men's and women's teams in 2007. Sheehan's experience as a golf writer, editor, course developer, and passionate student of the game will insure that Paterson's approach remains alive and well at Yale.

William Sperry Beinecke
Benefactor of the Yale Golf Course

A passion for the game, a lifelong commitment to the University, and the great success of The Sperry and Hutchinson Company (S & H Green Stamps) have led William S. "Bill" Beinecke (Class of 1936) to be the principal benefactor of the Yale Golf Course for more than a half century.

Bill Beinecke attended Westminster School and Phillips Academy before he came to Yale. Although he had his first golf lesson at age eleven at Baltusrol, he really learned to play golf at the Madison Golf Club in Madison, New Jersey and the Morris County Golf Club in Convent, New Jersey. At Yale he played quite a bit of recreational golf, although, as a student, he was unaware that the varsity golf team won intercollegiate championships in 1933 and 1936. After graduation he went to Columbia Law School and graduated in 1940. In 1941 he joined the US Navy and served in the destroyer fleets of both the Atlantic and Pacific theatres. He was involved in nine Pacific battles, was awarded the Bronze Star, and was discharged as a lieutenant commander in 1945. Even during the war he found a few opportunities to play golf. After the war he helped found the law firm of Casey, Beinecke and Chase in New York City. In 1952, Beinecke joined The Sperry and Hutchinson Company, co-founded by his great-uncle Thomas Sperry, as its general counsel. He became president in 1960, and later, chairman. He retired in 1980.

Beinecke has played golf all over the world with many fascinating people. One of his most memorable rounds was at the Cotton Bay Club on the island of Eleuthera in the Bahamas. There, he and his friend John T. (Jack) Connor played with Jess Sweetser and Watts Gunn, who had played together on the Walker Cup team. Gunn was a friend of Bobby Jones and a fellow member of the East Lake Golf Club in Atlanta. Jones persuaded Gunn to go to the Amateur Championship with him at Oakmont in 1925. They ended up meeting in the finals, the only time this has

William Sperry Beinecke

happened between two members of the same club. (Jones won.) Bill Beinecke and his son, John, and, later, his grandson, Barrett, have played many times in the Father and Son Golf Association championship. Now in his 90s, Bill Beinecke still plays some golf at Baltusrol, at Eastward Ho! (in Chatham on Cape Cod), at Gulf Stream (in Delray Beach, Florida), and at Yale.

For all of Bill Beinecke's success in business, his greatest recognition has come from his philanthropy and community service work in the fields of education, the arts, environmental preservation, and equal opportunity. The Beinecke

Rare Book and Manuscript Library at Yale, given by the generation before Bill, is a world-renowned collection and scholarly center, and the Beinecke name is on several endowed academic chairs. Beinecke was awarded an honorary LLD degree in 1986, and both he and his daughter, Frances, have served as Fellows of the Yale Corporation.

At the golf course, however, one must search to find the Beinecke name, although the stamp of his generosity is everywhere. On the left of the first tee is a small bronze plaque commemorating his 1968 gift of the course's first, in-ground, irrigation system. Then-president, Kingman Brewster, thought the money should have been spent for academic purposes, but Beinecke insisted that it be used to improve the course. It was an enormous boon to the health of the course, although it was dedicated quite modestly by a round of golf that Beinecke played with Ellis Knowles, his son Jimmy, and several others. One may also notice a small plaque at the entrance to the golf cart storage building that acknowledges Beinecke's 1972 gift of this building, designed by architect Herbert Newman, and additional funds for carts and cart paths. The present clubhouse was dedicated in 1984 as a gift from Bill Beinecke's Prospect Hill Foundation. It too was designed by Herb Newman and replaced the remodeled and enlarged "shack" that Beinecke remembered affectionately from his undergraduate days at the course. The original

Plaque on the first tee commemorating the 1968 gift of the first inground irrigation system by William S. Beinecke

William W. Kelly

double-facing fireplace was retained from the earlier structure, and an oil painting of William S. Beinecke '36 hangs over the fireplace in the entrance hall. The Beinecke name is most prominently visible in the main hall, where the winners of the annual William S. Beinecke Alumni-Member Guest Invitational Golf Tournament are displayed. This event was started in 1975 by David Paterson to honor Beinecke's many contributions to Yale golf and remains one of the highpoints of the annual calendar. Fittingly, in 2003, Bill's son, John Beinecke, and his partner, Chuck Lobdell, were the low gross winners.

William T. Lee
Eleven-time Yale Golf Club champion

The Connecticut State Amateur golf championship tournament was first held in 1899. Since then, only six players have won it three times. The Reverend William T. Lee is one of them, winning at the Yale Golf Course in 1975, at the New Haven Country Club in 1979, and at the Hartford Golf Club in 1990. He has won the championship of the Yale Golf Club eleven times. No one else can match that record.

Lee learned to play the game in La Marque, Texas, at the Galco Country Club with his father, mother, brother, and sister. He graduated from Augustana College in Rock Island, Illinois in 1966. As a senior, he was president of the student body, Phi Beta Kappa, and captain of the golf team. He was selected for the All-American college division golf team. He was the individual winner of the College Conference Championship as a freshman and sophomore. The thirty-six-hole score of 138 that he posted in 1964 still stands as an NCAA record. As a senior, Lee finished seventh in the NCAA college division championship.

In 1966 Lee came to New Haven to attend the Yale Divinity School. The academic year, 1968-1969 found him in Los

Angeles for his internship. To help with expenses, Lee caddied for Rocky Thompson in the L.A. Open. He received a Masters of Divinity degree in 1970 and a Masters of Sacred Theology in 1971. Lee started studying for a doctoral degree in 1972 but stopped when he was ordained. He served as the pastor of the Emanuel Lutheran Church in New Haven from 1972 until he retired in 2006.

From 1966 until 1975 Lee played golf only recreationally at the Yale course. Conditions were different then, with no in-ground watering system, no carts, and one hit — and retrieved — his own balls on the practice range. Lee found that the "course demanded creativity" and played hard and fast, "like a Scottish course."

In 1975 he returned to competition and won his first state amateur title. The competition was held at Yale, and Lee recalls that play was stopped several times because of noise from the construction site of the present clubhouse. The new clubhouse, the addition of a watering system, carts, and outside play have changed the character of the course.

The 1970s and 1980s were busy times for Reverend Lee. In addition to being a father, pastor, pilot, and golfer, he was also active in the community. He took flying lessons and received his license in 1974. Lee served on the New Haven City Council from 1974 to 1976. He failed in his run for the state legislature, but he was the director of the New Haven Welfare Department from 1980 to 1990. He directed a television program for the Connecticut Council of Churches and advised the national council on TV programming. In 1990 Lee started a home for at-risk teenage girls.

Even with all these activities, Lee won the state amateur again in 1979 and 1990. He qualified five times for the US Amateur, five times for the Mid Amateur, three times for the British Amateur, and twice for US Senior Amateur. He has played with professionals, such as Brad Faxon, Billy Andrade,

Jay Siegel, Joey Sindelar, Bob Tway, and John Schroeder. He caddied in PGA tournaments for Julius Boros and Tommy Bolt after they had won the US Open. He was scheduled to caddie for Tony Lema on the day that Lema died in a plane crash. Many would rate Bill Lee the best player at Yale from 1966 to 2006. He believes that honor ought to go to Peter Teravainen, Bob Heintz, and Heather Daly-Donofrio.

Bill Lee winning his third Connecticut Amateur in 1990

After another decade-long absence from competition, Lee came back in 2005 to finish as runner-up in the state Senior Amateur, and he qualified for several national tournaments. The 2005 CSGA Media Guide noted that "the state's elite golfers will enjoy the Rev.'s return and his boyish enthusiasm. And who knows, maybe there's another championship in his bag." That came in 2008 when Lee won the CSGA Senior Amateur to become only the third person to win both the Amateur and Senior Amateur. Bill Lee ended the year by finishing his two-year term as Captain of the CSGA Team, and by being named Senior Player of the Year. Best of all, he was inducted into the Connecticut Golf Hall of Fame.

Peter Teravainen
1978 team captain and international professional tour player

When Scotsman David Paterson came to Yale as the golf coach in 1975, Peter Teravainen (Class of 1978) was a freshman from Duxbury, Massachusetts and the best player on the team. He was named to All-American teams in 1976, 1977, and 1978 and was team captain in his senior year. With Coach Paterson's encouragement Teravainen set out as a golf professional in 1979.

His career is certainly proof that golf is an international game. Teravainen was unsuccessful in qualifying for the US PGA Tour, but he has played in six national open championships, won on four different tours around the world, and won three national championships: the Singapore (where he lives) PGA Championship in 1989 and 1991, the Czech Open in 1995, and the Japan Open in 1996. In the Japan Open, a hole-in-one afforded him the opportunity to donate the $25,000, MasterCard-Tom Watson Prize to charity. He chose to give it to the United Nations University.

In June 2001 Teravainen returned to Yale for the celebration of David Paterson's twenty-five years as coach. Coach Paterson asked Peter to talk at the reunion. Here are some of his remarks.

> *Golf can be a fun game, but if you are going to play it professionally for more than two decades you better have a sense of humor. I posed a question to the foreign Pros on the Japanese Tour last month, and they gave me a lot of help in solving it. I asked, "Which American Professional Golfers have wins on the European, Australian, Asian, Japanese Tours and a Major title?" With all this brain power working on a useless bit of trivia, we came up with a player who started his career outside the US and was able to win on these*

four tours and later a major. Payne Stewart accomplished this feat. I offered myself as another player who had achieved wins on four different tours and a major. We all had a good laugh, but everyone on the Japanese Tour considers the Japan Open "The" Japanese Major to win. When you are a player, a ten-year exemption gets your attention.

Peter Teravainen, circa 1978

1980 was my first full year as a golf professional, and I was on the US PGA Tour, but I must say I wasn't ready. One person who deserves a medal was my Tuesday practice round partner, Mike Donald. We lost every single Tuesday, but he didn't give up on me. He must have been a little bit relieved when I lost my card, so he could find a new partner for the practice round money games. In 1981 Mike was rewarded for his patience. His new partner was a rookie by the name of Fred Couples. The start of my international career resulted from a conversation at the score board at the 1981 US Tour School. I missed by one shot, and there was no Nike or Buy.com Tour back then. One of the Pros told me that the European Tour was giving out playing status to the top 15 players who missed out at the US Tour School. The European Tour is truly a global tour. It has tournaments in Asia, Australia, Africa, Middle East, and South America.

I learned a lot at Yale, but now I would be starting my advanced degree in Economics. My strongest memory of the week in Tunisia was a waiter at the hotel restaurant asking *me if I was a capitalist. Having a total of $3,000 of capital didn't stop me from stating that "Of course I am a capitalist." Luckily, I didn't get food poisoning that week. The next three tournaments were in Madrid, Sardinia, and Paris. And all roads went through Rome. Keeping expenses down was a major consideration for nearly all the players in the 1980s. The tournament purses were very small. The tour travel agent organized a cheap air ticket on Alitalia, so we wasted a lot of time making connections in Rome. On one of the overnight layovers in Rome, my roommate was the eccentric Mac O'Grady. That night he spent hours telling me swing theories from the book "The Golfing Machine." The next day I asked the travel agent not to assign us as roommates anymore. Maybe that was a mistake. When Mac made it on the US, Tour the other players voted his swing the best. In the 1990s, Mac became a consultant to some of the top players in the game.*

My roommate in Sardinia and much of my first year on the European Tour was able to give me an insight into America Civil Rights in the 1960s and how it related to professional golf. The US PGA didn't rescind the "Caucasian only" rule until 1961. My roommate, Rafe Botts, was one of a handful of black professionals who were finally able to play full time on the US Tour in the 1960s. But it still wasn't easy or completely fair. Now we live in a different world. The Supreme Court stepped in and changed rules fundamental to running a golf tournament. Where was the Supreme Court 40 years ago when they were truly needed to help make the PGA Tour a fair workplace?

US Tour player, Jim Thorpe, was playing in the Nigerian Open that year. Nigeria was probably one of the toughest places I have ever played golf. I didn't feel comfortable, and the putting surface, a mixture of sand and oil, gave me problems. Both Jim and I decided that we wouldn't be going back to Nigeria. I had played with Jim's brother, Chuck Thorpe, on the mini-tours in Florida. When Chuck heard I was from Yale he suggested that we work together. He said that with his brains and my bankroll we would form a strong partnership. When I told Chuck the extent of my bankroll, he withdrew the offer. That is still the only business opportunity I ever received because of my Yale connection.

I definitely wouldn't have become one of the answers to the earlier trivia question if it weren't for my wife, Veronica. My first big win in Singapore came weeks after the birth of our daughter, Taina. The Chinese say a baby brings luck. In fact, my biggest win, the 1996 Japan Open happened only because Veronica did all the groundwork that would allow me to get a Japanese visa. I wasn't going to play because I don't have much patience for government red tape. After I won, she told me it was her dream for me to change from Europe to Japan. The Japanese Tour wasn't even on my radar screen until I won the Japan Open. The travel to Europe was starting to wear me out, so it was nice to cut my fourteen hours commuting time in half. Even though she has never played golf, Veronica has become quite an expert. I asked her to remember her caddie experiences, and I found out she got more conversation out of Nick Faldo than I ever did. In 1989 in a heavy downpour at Monte Carlo, Nick commiserated with her as she was getting wet and her player was rushing on up ahead with the umbrella. Nick asked why she caddied for such a jerk. She replied, "What to do? He's my husband." Later that summer would be Veronica's last week as a caddie, and what a tournament to finish on — The Open at Royal Troon. Early in the week the front of the practice range was used, and it had a downhill lie. One player was working on his long irons beside me but was having problems and left the range a little disappointed with his swing. Veronica asked, "Who was that old guy? He nearly fell down after every *swing." It was Arnold Palmer. In the third round we were paired with Jack Nicklaus, and I was extremely nervous. Veronica chatted merrily with Jack quite often during the round and told me he is a nice player to be paired with. I smiled weakly and prayed the tightness in my body was not a heart attack about to happen.*

In 1991 a University of Pennsylvania alumnus, Michael Bamberger, caddied for me and he produced a pretty good book, "To the Linksland." People have come up to me all over the world and asked me to sign it. One year I was on the first tee at North Berwick in Scotland getting ready to qualify for The Open, and an old Yalie and his wife ambled out and asked me to sign their favorite book. They enjoyed taking a Scottish holiday every year. I asked Michael not to mention one of my swings in his book. My most well-known swing even had a name. It was called the "Whiplash," and, in hindsight, I'm glad Michael ignored my request to keep it out of his book. For the record, my first whiplash was at the Swiss Open in 1982. I received a lot of good natured ribbing over the years from the other players because of this swing that recoiled tremendously from the follow through position.

In 2006 the fifty-year-old Teravainen tried to qualify for the PGA Senior Tour. He fell short and again turned to the European Senior Tour. He remains Yale's only international professional golfer.

Heather Daly-Donofrio
Varsity player and coach, LPGA Tour player

So far, only one Yale graduate, Heather Daly-Donofrio (Class of 1991), has won a professional golf tournament on a major United States golf tour. In 2001 she won the First Union Betsy King Classic on the LPGA tour. Then she did it again in 2004, winning The Mitchell Company Tournament of Champions.

How she got to Yale and became a golf champion is an interesting story.

At age eight Heather Daly came to compete at the Payne
Whitney Gym pool as a member of the Norwalk Water Rats.
Later that day she informed her mother that she was going to
attend college at Yale. At thirteen she was swimming there
regularly as a member of the New Haven Swim Club team,
coached by Yale's Frank Keith. At age fifteen, she taught
herself to play golf by reading instruction books and by trial
and error, using a set of aluminum-shafted clubs that her
uncle had bought at a tag sale. She played for the Roger
Ludlow High School team, coached by a non-golfer. True to
her word Daly applied only to Yale, where she had been
recruited for both the swim and golf teams.

At Yale most of Daly-Donofrio's time outside the classroom was spent on the golf course. She was still learning to
play, without instruction, by just
playing. Often she would not
make it back to Berkeley College
for dinner. After two years, she
quit the swim team to concentrate on golf. She was not the best
player on the team that won the
Ivy League championship two
times, but as coach of both the
men's and women's team, David
Paterson saw more potential and
predicted that someday she
"would be a great player." After
one semester of her junior year
spent at Oxford, Daly-Donofrio
"learned how to study," and
returned to a straight-A senior
year and cum laude graduation.

Yale Athletics Archives

Heather Daly-Donofrio at Yale

Instead of going to law school, she decided to give professional golf a try for one or two years.

Winning the Connecticut Women's Amateur Championship in 1992 and 1993 was encouraging. Not so encouraging was working for $5 an hour, cleaning clubs and carts at Jonathan's Landing Golf Club in Jupiter, Florida, while playing "mini-tour" events, and trying to qualify for the LPGA Tour. Even though Daly-Donofrio won four mini-tour events over the next five years, she "went broke several times." In 1997 to have "a paying job with benefits," she accepted the offer to coach the Yale women's team. At the end of that year she qualified for the LPGA Tour.

For three years Daly-Donofrio played 20-24 LPGA events and coached Yale to the Ivy League championship in 1997. In 1998 she and Raymond Howell were married. By 2000 Daly-Donofrio "was exhausted by her various roles" and gave up coaching, because "the girls weren't getting what they had signed up for." She was elected by her peers to the LPGA Player Executive Committee in 2003 and became the LPGA Tour president in 2005. At that time she was also co-chair of the search committee to select a new LPGA commissioner. Also in 2005 she received the William and Mousie Powell Award, "which recognizes an LPGA player who, in the opinion of her playing peers, through her behavior and deeds best exemplifies the spirit, ideals and values of the LPGA." The late Mousie Powell, wife of Hollywood legend William Powell, had been a supporter of the LPGA since the 1950s and donated this award in 1986. Since then, some of the other winners have been Kathy Wentworth, Nancy Lopez, Pat Bradley, JoAnne Carner, Betsy King, Judy Rankin, Meg Mallon, Suzy Whaley, and Juli Inkster. The new commissioner, Carolyn F. Bivens, and the executive committee made changes in the tour structure and administration during 2006 that Heather believes assure a bright future for the LPGA.

Heather's future also became clearer in 2006. Her first child, Hannah Daly Howell was born. For those who have assumed that her married name was Daly-Donofrio, let the record show that Heather Daly took the name Daly-Donofrio at age twenty to honor her maternal grand-father. With her presidency behind her and a three-year exemption from qualifying, thanks to her Tour Championship victory, she and Hannah returned to the tour full time in 2007 (with the rotating help of her husband and mother). Her winnings in the first four events put her career winnings to more than one million dollars in her tenth

Heather Daly-Donofrio, winner of the 2004 Mitchell Group LPGA Tournament of Champions

year on tour. As she began 2007, she didn't expect to play beyond her period of exemption, and, she said, "At some point I wouldn't mind working in sports marketing or for the Tour."

The year 2009 might be Daly-Donofrio's final year on the LPGA Tour, but Yale will still be represented. Jeehae Lee came to Yale from South Korea and graduated in 2006. Like Heather Daly-Donofrio, she was not the best player of her cohort, but she contributed to Yale teams that won the Ivy League Cham-pionship twice, in 2003 and 2006. She was the low amateur in the 2006 Connecticut Women's Open, but, by her own account, she managed only a mediocre record as a professional on the Duramed Futures tour in 2007 and 2008. She was ranked 78th on that tour, but persistence and hard work paid off. Surprising everyone but herself, she won one of the coveted twenty spots on the 2009 LPGA Tour, with a strong finish at Q-School in December of 2008.

Bob Heintz
Three-time Ivy League champion and PGA Tour player

Bob Heintz (Class of 1992) regained his PGA Tour card for the fourth time and will be back in the big show in 2009. This is how he got there.

Heintz was born on Long Island, where his parents had taken their first teaching jobs. However, their jobs were eliminated when student enrollment fell, and at age five Heintz moved to Cape Coral, Florida. There he learned to play golf by tagging along with his father and grandmother. He played a number of sports in high school, but after suffering a minor knee cartilage tear during basketball season, Heintz decided to focus on golf instead of baseball in the spring, because the strain of being a catcher would have been difficult. As a senior, Heintz led the golf team and held the lowest scoring average for high school golfers in Pinellas County.

Because he visited his grandparents on Long Island every summer, he wanted to return to the northeast for college. He applied to Yale after being "lightly recruited for basketball." He was skeptical of his admission chances until he went for his alumni interview near his home in Florida. Luckily the interviewer was very happy to meet the young man, whose athletic career he had followed in the papers and with whose father he had taught on Long Island.

Heintz came to play basketball, but after seeing the golf course the summer before he entered and the scores posted by college players, he decided to try out for the golf team. "I first met David Paterson in a classroom along with twenty-

five other guys who were also responding to a flyer
announcing tryouts for the golf team. We filled out a ques-
tionnaire, and I said I was a 4 handicap. At the course the first
time, I was completely intimidated and didn't break 80." Even
so, Coach Paterson let him practice with the team that fall and
then invited him on the spring trip to the West Coast. Heintz
had become discouraged with the basketball program, so he
decided to concentrate on being "two-sided," a student and a
golfer, for the next three years.

   Heintz scheduled
all his classes before
11 A.M. and spent
each afternoon at the
course. The people at
the course, Peter
Pulaski, Toni Corvi,
Mike "Mow" Moran,
and Brad Saunders,
were his "family" and
the course his "sanc-
tuary." But his main
inspiration   was
Coach Paterson, who
told him at the begin-
ning of his junior year
that   he   should
consider being a
professional golfer.
Heintz thought he
was joking, but the
turning point came
that spring at the
Wofford Invitational
tournament at the

Yale Athletics Archives

Bob Heintz, 1992

Country Club of South Carolina. Heintz came in fourth with a 68 on the last day. He beat Chris Patton, then the US Amateur champion, and many other southern collegiate golfers who hadn't spent the winter in New Haven. He won the Ivy League individual championship three years in a row at Bethpage Black (by 13 strokes as a senior). Also as a senior, he made the Academic All-American Team with a 3.20 GPA. He reports that "the NCAA called to make sure the GPA hadn't been rounded-up to meet the minimum requirement of 3.2."

Just before graduation Heintz was working on job applications when David Paterson told him, "You have the rest of your life to 'get a job'; you're going to try professional golf." His parents had always supported him, and now they did again, and so did his soon-to-be wife, Nancy. The financial support he needed came from Paterson's network of friends and from Heintz's friends and family.

Thirty thousand dollars per year for the period from 1992 to 1994 allowed him to play the mini tours around Orlando Florida. Even when he won a couple of events, however, the prize money he returned to his investors was less than fifty per cent of their investment. He went to the PGA qualifying tournament in 1994. By making it to the final stage, he qualified for the Nike (now Nationwide) Tour. Coach Paterson had told him in 1992 that to succeed as a Pro he would "have to cure his hook and learn to play a fade." He did that, without instruction, by "pretending he was Freddie Couples." But, in the final stage of qualifying in 1994, "pretending broke down." This continued on the Nike Tour where he was "out of his element and a complete failure." By 1996 his investors were losing interest in losing money, and Nancy was pregnant. Heintz quit professional golf.

Heintz took a real job, with Raymond James Financial, in the back office "counting peanuts" for $21,000 a year. Six months later David Paterson arrived for a Christmas visit.

Seeing that Heintz had gained thirty pounds, he declared, "You look like shit. Why are you not playing golf anymore?" When Heintz explained the situation, the only question Paterson asked was, "How much money do you need?" Within three months Paterson had raised the needed $35,000, from eighteen investors (including three Catholic nuns who split one share between them). That money was supplemented, as it had been in previous years, by Heintz working as an assistant golf coach at the University of South Florida in Tampa. By 1998 he was on the Hooters Tour, and his investors were getting a return on their now $50,000 annual investment. He was second on the money list (with over $100,000), which earned him a $50,000 bonus.

Heintz had conditional status on the Nike Tour in 1999, so he had to decide whether he would play there or stay on the Hooters Tour. His Hooters 1998 $50,000 "bonus" was paid out in installments of $1,200 for each Hooters Tour event he entered. His very practical mother advised against his plan to play the Nike Tour (with no such guarantee). Heintz's response to his mother was, "I didn't get a Yale degree and turn Pro to play the Hooters Tour. It was to play the PGA Tour, and I can't get there from the Hooters." Two weeks later he won the Nike Tour event at Shreveport and $42,000. Later that year he won the Nike Tour Championship at Dothan Alabama in a play-off with Marco Dawson, who had played the Hogan Tour event at Yale in the 1980s. Heintz entered the tournament at sixteenth on the money list, which would have gotten him directly to the final stage of PGA Q School. A good check would have moved him to fifteenth or higher and qualified him for the 2000 PGA Tour directly. Winning was even better.

As a Yale graduate and rookie on the 2000 PGA Tour, Heintz attracted the attention of *Sports Illustrated*. He agreed to write an online weekly diary. It was immensely enjoyable, but he stopped the time-consuming series after nine months. It was difficult, Heintz admitted, to "relive his failures weekly," and he also was surprised and discouraged by some "painful" negative feedback from critical fans, amidst the overwhelmingly positive responses. He led the PGA Tour in putting in 2002. Impressive, but he later said that it really meant that he was not hitting greens in regulation and he missed sixteen of twenty-one cuts. Since then Heintz has been on the Nationwide Tour in 2003, 2004, 2006, and 2008 and back on the PGA Tour in 2005 and 2007 for the second time, with no thoughts of a job at Raymond James.

Yale Athletics Archives

Bob Heintz on the 2008 PGA Tour

Bob and Nancy Heintz and their three children now live in Dunedin, Florida. When at home, he occasionally plays the Dunedin Country Club (which was the first site of the PGA headquarters), but usually he plays at the Countryside Country Club in Clearwater, which he represents on tour, and where he is a member. Heintz was very excited about returning to the PGA Tour in 2007 because he believed that he was ready this time, with his swing tools in place and an instructor keep him in groove. He was using the same caddie, Jeff Dean, a fifty-two-year-old country boy from "LA" (lower

Alabama)—a bachelor who sold a few restaurants in 1999 to try the caddie life. He had earned $50,000 with Heintz in 2005. Dean's demeanor is laidback, which helps Heintz to "de-stress." And Heintz could study the focus of Tiger Woods and other stars in dealing with the "circus of the tour." He could use the fitness trailer and the trainers who are provided on the PGA to be ready to play no matter when his tee time. Finally he singles out his wife, Nancy, as a huge part of his team. Never once, he says appreciatively, has she "told [him] he should be doing something else." Nancy Heintz is very astute in analyzing his swing and game plan. Together they work out a plan of attack and set goals for the smallest detail of that plan. It's not just "one shot at a time, it's even how do I breath over this putt."

It did seem to be working early in the 2007 season. Heintz had played in 233 PGA and Nationwide Tour events prior to 2007, with an average income per event of $4,964. In twenty-seven PGA and two Nationwide Tour events in 2007 he aver-aged $22,400. However, competition is intense, and PGA pros are playing for a lot of money. He failed to retain his PGA card for 2008 because he ranked 125th on the money list. In 2008 he fell to 169th while playing on both Tours. Happily, his fortunes have turned again, and Heintz ended 2008 by regaining his PGA Tour card for 2009 at Q-School. His career earnings now top two million dollars. That certainly is better than he was doing at Raymond James, and the story isn't over yet.

Gary Benerofe and Steve Gray
1999 and 2005 team captains

Gary Benerofe (Class of 1999) and Steve Gray (Class of 2005) tell similar stories. They were both good junior golfers who were not thinking about Yale. Benerofe was living in

Westchester County, New York, and preparing to attend Duke or the University of Michigan, when Coach Paterson called. Gray was in Kansas City and planning to attend San Diego State University and later play golf professionally, when the call came.

Neither Benerofe nor Gray knew why they were invited to visit Yale but they came to take a look. Benerofe remembers that he was "sold on attending Yale ... after a raucous weekend with the golf team." Gray came and toured the course when it was covered with snow, and met some of the team members. He was "drawn to the university, and changed his plans, with the encouragement of his grandmother."

In Benerofe's first year on the team (1995), there were only ten players and half of them were freshman. By his senior year, the team's success as Ivy League champions in 1996 and 1997 and strong recruiting resulted in twenty-five to thirty players competing for the six tournament slots. As a senior he was elected captain, even though he received the second highest number of votes. The 1998 captain and his roommate, Scott Brinker, had been a junior when he was elected. He was reelected in 1999, but requested that Coach Paterson select the person who had received the second highest number of votes "so that someone else could have the great experience."

Benerofe received an MBA from UCLA in 2005. He is now working in his family's real estate business, Benerofe Properties. He reports that he "recently picked the game back up and loves it again, like I did when I was thirteen." He continues to value the role that Coach Paterson played in his life. Benerofe says that Paterson "was like a second father to me and many others."

In 2006 Steve Gray was not playing golf professionally, as he had once planned; he was working on his Master's degree in Organizational Psychology at Columbia. He was also assisting Coach Paterson with the team on weekends. In 2003,

Gray had been a member of the team that won the Ivy Championship and was team captain in 2005. For Gray the best memories come from the team's spring trips: first to Scotland, where they played Troon and St. Andrews, then to California, where they played Pebble Beach, Spyglass, Cypress Point, and Riviera. As a junior, he was able to play Colonial and Hilton Head and in his senior year, some Florida courses. Gray observed that "You can see that after more than thirty years, Coach has made some great contacts." He described "Coach" as "old school": "He can be harsh and a disciplinarian, though never on the course. He has some interesting metaphors and kernels of wisdom." Coach Paterson was as influential as many of Gray's professors and, "compared to other college coaches, much more open to his players' personal and academic growth."

Women's varsity golf arrives

1969 was the first year that women were admitted as undergraduates at Yale, and within several years, they organized club teams in field hockey, fencing, and several other sports. In 1972, Lawrie Mifflin and Sandy Morse were the first women to sit on the honorary Yale fence as sports captains. Indeed, as co-captains of the field hockey team, they were actually the first ever co-captains in Yale athletic history. After Chris Ernst, a two-time Olympian rower, led the Women's Crew in a famous "strip-in" protest against Yale's lack of athletic facilities for women, the University moved aggressively to expand opportunities and equalize facilities for female undergraduate athletes.

Women's golf was one of the last sports to emerge as a varsity sport. David Paterson was a motivating force, and he served as its first coach from 1980 to 1993. The women played their first match as a varsity team on April 10, 1981 at the Yale course, losing to Rutgers with a three-person team captained by Andrea Francis, with Mary Lee Rhodes and Teddy Strain.

Darci Wilson took over for Paterson as coach for a year in 1993-1994, and then Amy Huether led them from 1994 to 1997. The Ivy League did not hold its first women's championship in golf until April 1997. Playing at Bethpage (Long Island) Golf Course, the Yale team won convincingly by thirty-four strokes. Yale also dominated the first All-Ivy team; Charity Barras, Natalie Wong, and Chawwadee Rompothong were named to three of the seven places. The individual title in 1997 was won by Princeton's Mary Moan, who capped her outstanding

Women's Varsity Golf Team, 1997 Ivy League Champions. Back from left: Rachel Brakeman, Margret Bell, Ilona Paulin, Charity Barras, Emily Johnson, Coach Amy Huether; front from left: Chawwadee Rompothong, Natalie Wong, Tiffany Wolhfiel, Katie Fisher

undergraduate career by becoming Princeton's first All-American in women's golf.

Heather Daly-Donofrio graduated in the Class of 1991 after playing under Coach Paterson and went on to play on the professional Futures Tour. In 1997, she became the women's team coach and took the team to its second consecutive Ivy title in a much more competitive tournament. After the first of two days, Yale was tied with Princeton, with team totals of 325, and the title came down to the final hole of the final twosome, when Yale's Natalie Wong made par to beat Princeton's Laura Gillmore by a stroke. Wong's 154 for the two rounds also gave her the individual title.

Princetonian Mary Moan took over as coach in 2000 and recruited many successful players as the level and intensity of play continued to rise. In 2007, Chawwadee Rompothong returned to her alma mater. After graduating in 2000, Rompothong played on the Futures Pro Tour for two and one-half years, before becoming a teaching professional at Pinehurst (North Carolina). She moved back to Connecticut to teach at a private club and was named women's team coach in 2007.

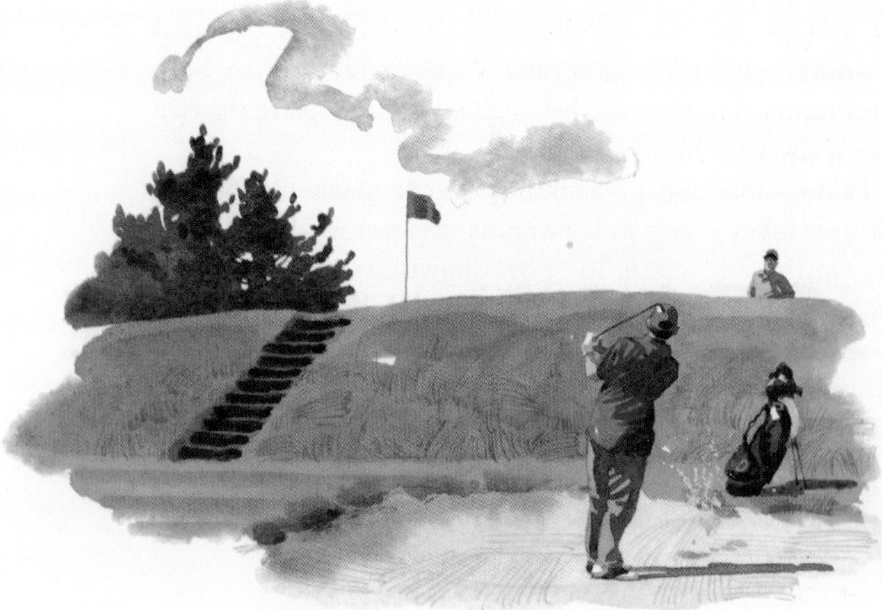

Into the 21st Century
The Era of Thomas Beckett, Peter Pulaski, and Scott Ramsay

In 1983 Ben Crenshaw came to Yale to admire the work of Raynor and Macdonald. Touring the course, he became increasingly alarmed and saddened and was moved to write then-President Bart Giamatti, calling attention to the sorry state of what he termed a "national treasure." But nothing changed for a decade until Tom Beckett arrived as the new Director of Athletics. Since 2006, the Yale Golf Course has been rated the best university course in the country. Much of the credit for that belongs to Tom Beckett, Peter Pulaski, and Scott Ramsay, whose collective vision and efforts have moved Yale golf into the twenty-first century and restored the course to the front ranks of American courses.

Thomas Beckett
University Director of Athletics

At the University of Pittsburgh, Tom Beckett was a three-year letterman in basketball and baseball, and captain of the baseball team. He coached baseball at Pittsburgh and baseball and basketball at Butler Community College. He was associate athletic director at San Jose State and Stanford University before coming to Yale. After college he had been an infielder in the San Francisco Giants farm system. He took up golf after watching the San Francisco Giants baseball players (especially Willie Mays) hit balls at a driving range during spring training. When he went to work at Stanford University, he took lessons from the pro Larry O'Neil. At Stanford he developed an "appreciation for the game and what a good course can do for a university community."

When he came to Yale in 1994, he was shocked to find that the course he had heard so much about was in such poor condition. For a year he asked questions and studied. He found that the university was forcing the Athletics Department to "balance its books on the back of the golf course." That was changed, and an investment program in the course was begun, along with the development of an alumni support base. It took the turnover of four superintendents in ten years before "we were blessed with a superstar, a miracle worker, a genius and visionary, Scott Ramsay." What had been slowly coming together "then exploded," resulting in a restored and beautiful course.

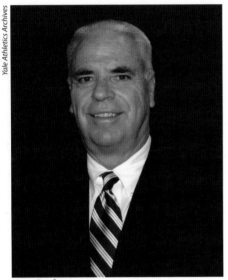

Tom Beckett, 2004

To ensure that those gains would not be lost, an endowment was created for the benefit of the golf program. Of equal importance was Beckett's ability to put together the team of then-Vice President John Pepper, Scott Ramsay, and Local 35 labor union leader, Bob Proto, to establish the most successful labor-management environment in the university. All these elements came into play when Yale hosted the 2004 NCAA Eastern Regional tournament. It was a great success, and the old-style course stood up to the best college players and their modern equipment. Only two of the final scores were under par. The winner, Bill Haas, was two-under par, whereas the regional winners at other courses were ten-under par or more. Beckett's wish list for the future includes a new practice facility and a bid to host a national championship. In a 2005 interview he said, "Along with the university and the alumni, I'm proud that my fingerprints are on the Yale golf course."

Peter Pulaski
Director of Golf and PGA professional

Peter Pulaski grew up in Stratford, Connecticut and was introduced to the game by his father and grandfather at Mill River Country Club. Mill River was well known for producing such great Connecticut amateur golfers as Ben Costello, John Downey, and John Ruby. During the 1930s and 1940s, Mill River was the site of the Shoreline Open, which was won by such legendary players as Tommy Armour, Gene Sarazen, Claude Harman, Ed "Porky" Oliver, and home club pro, Lou Galby.

Growing up, Pulaski could watch some of the best players in the state, and he learned the game under the tutelage of two accomplished professionals. Al Fuchs was Connecticut PGA Champion and Doug Dalziel won the Connecticut PGA and Connecticut Open Championships and played on the Senior PGA Tour. Pulaski played in the Connecticut State Junior Championship and was a semifinalist in the prestigious J. Borck Junior Championship. He played four years at Bunnell High School and captained the 1979 team under Connecticut Hall of Fame Coach, Pedro Tagatac. At Southern Connecticut State University, Pulaski played two seasons for Coach Tony Martone, a Yale Golf Club member. Southern's home course was Yale, and Pulaski remembers it as being "wet in the spring and brown and wild in the fall."

Pulaski began his professional career under Al Fuchs at Mill River and then was hired at Oronoque Village Country Club by Paul McGuire, under whom Pulaski first began giving golf lessons. Three years later he went to work for his old

Michael Marsland

Peter Pulaski (left) with Scott Ramsay (right)

mentor Doug Dalziel at Grassy Hill Country Club. Following his certification from the PGA of America Business Schools, Pulaski became the head professional when Dalziel left to join the Senior PGA Tour. "I caddied for Doug in a couple of events during the off-season; I learned so much just watching him."

In 1994, the year that Tom Beckett became Athletic Director, Pulaski came to Yale to work for David Paterson. Yale was bursting with activity in the area of golf instruction. Pulaski assisted Paterson with golf schools and camps and developed a large student base. "I really enjoy working with the Yale students; it's a lot of fun." Peter Pulaski also earned Connecticut Coaching Certification and coached at the high school level for three seasons.

In 2000 he became the Director of Golf and began focusing on golf course conditions. Working with Tom Beckett and Forrest Temple, Pulaski began scheduling quartile visits with the USGA agronomists to assess turf conditions. "I learned an awful lot about growing grass and what we needed to do here at Yale." First and foremost were tree removal and improved irrigation, and these were followed by the purchase of much needed maintenance equipment. The bunker restoration project started by Dave Paterson was completed, and a formal long term drainage plan developed. "It's such a big piece of property, we just keep picking away at it."

Pulaski is also proud of his efforts with Beckett, Temple, and course superintendent, Scott Ramsay, in working with members of the Local 35 Grounds Staff and with Union President Bob Proto to reach an agreement on increased golf course staffing and devise a job-sharing plan that uses students and off-season, dining hall workers from Yale. This pact has made a tremendous difference in the conditions of the golf course.

In 2003 Peter Pulaski was named Teacher of the Year by the Connecticut PGA, and in 2007 he was the Horton Smith Award Recipient. Pulaski has served two terms on the Connecticut PGA Board of Directors and on the Best Practices Education Committee at Yale University.

Scott Ramsay
Award-winning Course Superintendent

It was not until 2003 that Peter Pulaski was able to find the right person to execute the plan and reach the goals that Tom Beckett had set in 1994. Scott Ramsay already had twenty years of experience as a superintendent when he arrived at Yale in the fall of 2003. He left the Orchards Golf Club in South Hadley Massachusetts, after preparing it for the 2004 USGA Woman's Open Championship. Ramsay's father was in the landscaping business and his father-in-law has been the superintendent at the same golf course for more than forty years. Ramsay graduated from the University of Rhode Island with a degree in golf course management. He then worked as a superintendent at courses in Westchester County, Rhode Island, and Connecticut and served as a regional manager for the Arnold Palmer Management Company.

From his first visit in 1986 Ramsay was attracted to Yale, describing it as "unique, angular, with complex routing and big greens on a grand scale, having a great tradition and being part of a university." When he became superintendent, however, the situation was not so promising. The union staff had just gone on strike, so Ramsay used coaches, administrators, and golf club members to maintain the course for several weeks. Since then he has improved union-management relations. After only one year, he had a staff that was triple the size of the one when he arrived. Ramsay's staff consists of permanent full-time, full-time seasonal, and part-time seasonal (dining hall staff and students) employees, with sixteen to twenty employed at the peak. With this staff and new equipment, the greens can be cut daily and the fairways groomed every two to three days before play begins. From the beginning Ramsay's goal was to improve labor-management relations on the same scale as there were course improvements.

The bunker renovation and restoration project has been completed. Many fairway drainage problems have been corrected and more is planned. Approximately 2,500 trees have been removed around tees, greens, and along fairways, and the program is essentially completed. Ramsay is now pruning and managing "specimen trees" such as the Dawn Redwoods on the sixth, tenth, and eighteenth holes. These trees thrive in the swampy areas found there and were planted by the forestry school many years ago. The tree program has allowed the edges of many greens to be reclaimed resulting in several "false fronts." Scott hopes to restore the "double punch bowl" green on the third hole. This is all part of his desire to reclaim, preserve, and restore this great course that is so well "designed for match play."

Nearly every month Ramsay discovers something that had been hidden and adds to Yale's unique character. During his tenure, the course has moved up in rankings from unranked, to sixtieth, and now to forty-fifth of the Top One Hundred classic courses and is acknowledged as the number one university course in America. Ramsay's professional colleagues recognized his work by naming him National Golf Course Superintendent of the Year in 2006. However, he still insists there are many ways to improve the course. When we proposed that 2007 would be a good time to have a professional take photographs of the course, he and Pulaski brushed the idea aside, responding, "That's a good idea for 2010!"

Michael Marsland

Back row: Scott Ramsay, Golf Course Superintendent; Mike Moran, Master Gardener; Vin Capobianco, Senior Gardener; Ed DeFrank, Groundskeeper; middle row: Carmine Ferraro, Gardener; Larry Mingione, Gardener; Rob Colonna, Groundskeeper; front row: Jim Burgh, Senior Equipment Technician; Peter Gagliardi, Gardener and Shop Steward

Robert D. Grober
The sound of the golf swing

Bob Grober grew up in Westchester County, New York. At age
thirteen he started caddying, first at Briar Hall, then at Sleepy
Hollow, and finally at Mahopac Country Club. A Westchester
Golf Association caddie scholarship helped pay for his undergraduate education at Vanderbilt University. There he majored
in physics and mathematics and was a member of the golf
team. He competed in amateur golf events while working
towards his doctorate at the University of Maryland at College
Park. Grober qualified for the USGA Public Links Championship in 1986 and won the University of Maryland Club
Championship in 1988. Even as a standout varsity golfer at
Vanderbilt, he knew enough math and physics to calculate the
likelihood of making a living with his golf clubs — so he
became a physicist! He was a postdoctoral fellow at AT&T Bell
Laboratories before joining the Yale faculty in 1994, where he
is now the Frederick Phineas Rose Professor of Applied
Physics and Professor of Physics.

   He is still obsessed with the game. Soon after coming to Yale
he accidentally broke the shaft of a club, and it occurred to him
that something useful might fit in the hollow space of the shaft.
It took him ten years to figure out what that might be.

   Grober began with the belief that the key to a successful
golf swing is "reproducible tempo," generating identical
mechanics and speed on every swing, which few golfers except
professionals achieve. The professional is a "walking, talking,
breathing metronome." Grober figured out how to convert the
tempo of a club's swing into an audio soundscape by trans-
lating the speed of the swing into varying tones — low pitch
for slow, higher for faster. He developed a system of sensors,
microprocessor, and a transmitter that fits in the shaft of a
club and wirelessly broadcasts the "sound" of a swing tempo

to a headset. The golfer and/or instructor can use Sonic Golf to break down and "listen" to the components of a swing or to look at graphic representations of its forces and speed at crucial moments.

Yale University patented Sonic Golf and licensed it to the company Bob Grober set up to manufacture and market the device. They are now offering the system with the sensor already inserted into a club shaft, or a golfer can buy the sensor and put it into his own clubs. Golf Pride is manufacturing grips, which will allow easy insertion and removal of the device. The company is getting attention from teaching professionals and from science and golf media. Vijay Singh began using the device midway through the 2008 PGA season. He ended as the leading money winner (sixteen million dollars) with four tournament victories and the Fed Ex Cup championship. So, two decades after Bob Grober gave up any hope of becoming a golf professional, he thinks his chances of making money from the game are improving. But whether a financial success or not, he knows his own swing has improved. Grober admits, "I'd be lying if I said this wasn't about making me a better golfer!"

Bob Grober "listening" to his swing

Michael Marsland

The Yale Golf Association

Alumni have been encouraged to return for golf at a Yale venue for more than 100 years. Articles in the *Alumni Weekly* in the 1890s pointed out the ease of traveling from New York to New Haven by train and then by trolley to the first tee at the New Haven Golf Club. Matches between golf team members and alumni were reported in that era. Coach Ben Thomson began taking the team south in the spring, soon after he arrived at the Yale Golf Course in 1926. By the 1930s he was taking the team to Scotland. Who paid for these trips is not known. But, given the background of most of the players of that time, it would not have been a problem. After the Depression and World War II, students were more diverse and in need of financial support. A group of alumni formed the Yale Golf Association (Y.G.A.) to provide that support.

Before the 1970s, the Y.G.A. activities were simple and straightforward. On the first Saturday in May, the Yale Golf Association Annual Meeting and Lettermen's Reunion took place after a tournament matching alumni against team members. The event served as a reunion for team alumni and a fund-raising event. In addition, an appeal letter was sent out annually to all Yale Golf Club members, soliciting donations for the team's annual spring trip. The founders of the Y.G.A. are not known, but Widdy Neale, Burt Resnik, Alan Needleson, Arthur "Ace" Williams, and Dick Tettlebach were active members.

With the arrival of Coach David Paterson in 1975, the association became more active and focused. Board membership was expanded and there was stable leadership, with Herb Emmanuelson as president from 1963 to 1983 and Giles Payne from 1983 to 2003. David Paterson has been very successful raising funds from alumni, parents, and "Friends of Yale Golf." He started a second revenue-raising tournament, the "Scratch Cup," and later, a third tournament, the Yale Men's College-Am. It is played in the fall on the Friday preceding the Macdonald Cup.

Jim Rogers, the 1968 captain, was elected president of the association, along with several new board members in 2003.

A new mission statement was adopted that added preservation of the golf course itself to the association's traditional mission. The annual meeting and championship tournament were moved to Monday, and a foursome competition was added to the usual medal play event. Under the dynamic leadership of tournament director, Ian MacAllister (Class of 2000), the inaugural "Yale Golf Association Championship and Outing" in May 2004 was a huge success. It attracted 112 golfers, and its spirited auction and raffle were a historic fundraiser. Another event was added later that year, the Yale Women's College-Am, which like the men's, is now played in conjunction with the Yale Women's Fall Invitational tournament. The highlight of the day is a pre-round clinic given by an LPGA pro. During its first three years, through the efforts of board member Jack Curren, the Sea Island Resort has been the title sponsor. This event has also been an important revenue source. Julie Hansen (Class of 1988) joined Jim Rogers as co-president in 2005. After a very successful tenure, Rogers was replaced by Ian MacAllister at the end of 2006.

Yale's Clubhouses
1900, 1913, 1926, and 1984

Yale students, faculty, and alumni began playing golf at the New Haven Golf Club in 1895. Harry Vardon, the Open Champion, stopped there in April 1900, on his US tour to promote the new ball made by the Spalding Co., the "Vardon Flyer." He gave four exhibitions and played three matches in two days. He lost the first match, playing alone against the "better ball" of T. L. Cheney and T. Markoe Robertson, the Yale captain. Three days later, the *Hartford Courant* quoted him that it "had been a practice round, not a match." Vardon also declared that the course had "the best greens in the US." He may have given this interview sitting on the porch of the new clubhouse, built that year on the corner of Winchester Avenue and Division Street overlooking the first tee and the eighteenth green.

The clubhouse was designed by Robert H. Robertson, a prominent New York architect, active between 1890 and 1919 and a pioneer designer of skyscraper buildings. No doubt he took the time to design this small clubhouse because of his golfing passion; he was a member of the St. Andrew's Golf Club, a friend of John Reid, and the father of the Yale golf captain, T. M. Robertson. The only remaining record of the clubhouse is the architect's frontal elevation drawing. It shows a two-story bungalow-style building of perhaps 1,000 sq. ft. There was a small front porch, probably an office, and a common room downstairs and changing rooms upstairs. We do know that the men's chairs and women's chairs in the common room were selected by Mrs. William Lyon Phelps and Miss Sarah Whittlesey, the daughter of the first club

New Haven Museum

R. H. Robertson, Architect, 160 Fifth Avenue, New York City   ERECTED JANUARY, 1899

THE NEW HAVEN GOLF CLUB

May be reached by trolley from the N.Y., N.H. & H. R.R., the cars running
directly to the Grounds on Winchester Avenue.

president. Those chairs can be seen today at the New Haven
Museum.

During Vardon's second US tour in 1913, he and Ted Ray
lost to Francis Ouimet in a playoff for the US Open championship, characterized as "The Greatest Game Ever Played" by
Mark Frost in his book of that title. Vardon didn't visit the
Yale golfers, who had just moved to the Race Brook Country
Club in Orange. Vardon's third US tour, with his partner Ted
Ray, was in 1920. They played and won a match at Race Brook
against the Yale captain, Sidney Scott, and club member, Joe
Stein. At Race Brook, the members could repair to a large
three-story clubhouse with several dining areas, large men's
and women's locker rooms, a pro shop, several meeting rooms,
and a boardroom (known today as the Pryde Room). The clubhouse has recently been renovated but retains the exterior
native stone work and its early twentieth-century style.

The clubhouse at Race Brook Country Club in the 1920s

On April 15, 1926, the Yale golf course at the Ray Tompkins Memorial officially opened. Land acquisition and construction costs had been more than three-quarters of a million dollars. However, only $5,000 was spent on the clubhouse. It was a "log cabin style" building with a central double fireplace that heated two rooms, a pro shop and a changing room. There was a shower, but no lockers. Clothes were hung on hooks on the wall. Food service consisted of a hot dog and sandwich stand in the parking lot. It apparently was so Spartan that "arrangements were made with the Taft Hotel for a Club Room in the hotel free of charge for Patrons, Founders and Members of the course, and in addition for preference in engaging rooms. Guests of the Taft belonging to any organized golf club were to have the privilege of using the course from June 20th to September 15th each year upon payment of a greens fee of $5.00 per day." Sometime between 1951 and 1965, the clubhouse was updated; the pro shop was moved to the front of the building (facing the first tee), and a dining room and kitchen were installed. A flagstone patio offered diners a view

The cedar-shake clubhouse in the 1950s

The "lunch room" in the old clubhouse, circa 1975, with Zelma at the counter

of the scenic pond and the third and fourth holes. Harry Meusel noted in a report to the Athletics Department that "with the drilling of a new eighty-foot well at the clubhouse, drinking water no longer needs to be brought in, and pond-fish in the shower rooms were stories of the past."

As noted earlier, William S. Beinecke and his family have been very generous in their support of the golf course. This support began with the installation of the first automated in-ground watering system in 1968. Later they provided golf cart paths and a storage facility. Finally, in 1984, the most generous gift, The Prospect Hill Clubhouse, was completed. This single story, Modernist, wood frame structure, designed by Herbert Newman, was built on the footprint of the old clubhouse. It contains the 1926 fireplace, a large pro shop, several offices, a conference-team room, men's and women's locker rooms, a large modern kitchen, two dining areas indoors, and a patio. The "Garden Room" dining area is where the original patio was

Yale Athletics Archives

The lounge area of men's locker room in the old clubhouse, circa 1975. Note the fireplace that now is in the entrance hall of the Prospect Hill Clubhouse.

located. In 2007 the Prospect Hill Clubhouse received a new roof and siding, as did the cart barn. The clubhouse was repainted, and the ceilings and carpeting replaced. The team room was renovated to make a lounge area. The panoramic views from the new patio, the dining rooms and the lounge across the third fairway and the pond to the fourth fairway make this a perfect place to end the day at a great golf course.

Entrance to the Prospect Hill Clubhouse

The Prospect Hill Clubhouse from the fourth fairway

This aerial photograph is oriented north (top) to south (bottom). The prevailing wind in summer comes from the northwest, the upper left hand side of the photograph. Above the seventh and eighth holes stood the original water tower, from which gravity-flow irrigating pipes were run. The land beyond these holes was sold to the State of Connecticut for constructing the Wilbur Cross Parkway, which can be seen in the top left corner.

The main water course runs diagonally upwards from the bottom right of the photograph. It forms a pond at the base of the thirteenth tee where Harry Meusel built his small Japanese garden, then a small pond in front of the seventeenth tee, before running into the long narrow pond that is the water hazard between the third and fourth holes. From there it empties into Greist Pond, the body of water that must be carried at the ninth hole.

The original Greist estate forest land beyond the present ninth, tenth, and eleventh holes was where Raynor had proposed to build a second 18-hole course. This is no longer possible because some of that was sold for housing development, as visible on this photograph.

The Course, Hole by Hole

Many of the stories of Yale golf have been told, hole by hole, over the eighty-plus years at the present Yale course. We conclude with brief commentaries of some of the many highlights of these eighteen holes. We have drawn this sketch from a variety of sources, beginning with Charles Banks, who trod the entire preserve for months and supervised the construction from start to finish. He wrote a lengthy preview of the course for the *Yale Alumni Weekly* that appeared in its August 1925 issue. Banks's insightful descriptions remain so strikingly apt today and his language is so vivid that we begin the description of each hole with his words. We also draw on interviews with and commentaries by David Paterson, Peter Pulaski, and Scott Ramsay and on our own years of playing the course.

George Bahto's meticulous account of C.B. Macdonald, *The Evangelist of Golf: The Story of Charles Blair Macdonald* (Sleeping Bear Press, 2002), is an essential work of golf scholarship, and we are grateful to him and to Sleeping Bear Press for their permission to reproduce the hole drawings that he did for his own account of the Yale Golf Course in that book.

Total Course Yardage

	At present	In 1926
Long tees	6,749 Par 70	6,533 Par 70
Regular Tees	6,122 Par 70	6,099 Par 70
Short Tees	5,468 Par 70, W 71	5,577 Par 70

Yale students heading off the first tee in the 1950s

Current Course Rating/Slope

	Men	Women
Long tees	73.5/140	79.6/146
Regular tees	70.5/139	76.8/140
Short tees	66.9/128	70.8/125

As of the opening of the 2009 season, the following are the current record scores:

➤ Best women's score: 72 by Caroline Keggi in 1984 and Linda Kinnicutt in 1989

➤ Best men's amateur score: 64 by Tim Petrovic in 1987, playing for University of Hartford

➤ Best men's professional score: 63 by Jon Christian in 1992, playing in the New Haven Open of the Ben Hogan Tour (now the Nationwide Tour)

No. 1 Eli
410 yards, 383 yards, 350 yards, par 4

Charles Banks in 1925:

> *The play of the long and the bold may hug the woods to the right with increased water carry but shorter total distance to the hole and an easier second. The greens at Yale are so huge there can easily be two different styles of greens on the same hole. The green is a huge double green of the Road Hole type on the right and a punchbowl on the left set into a bit of a hollow bunkered left and right. The play to the left half of the green is over a deep bunker about the front and left side of the green, requiring a lofted ball. The play to the right of the green is a direct shot to the high shoulder of the approach with a kick in to the green. The right half of the green has a deep bunker all along the right side but a clear approach permitting a run up. It is evident that the play of the second shot is considerably dependent upon the placing of the first shot.*

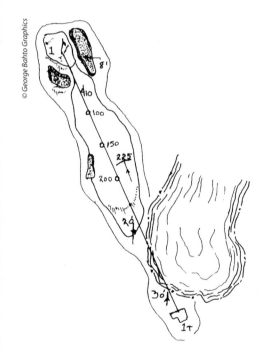

The first drive at Yale is certainly intimidating, standing on the elevated tees and looking over the corner of Greist Pond at the severe upslope that begins the fairway. A long drive is needed to carry the water and the fairway to avoid a blind second shot. A bunker guards the landing area's left side, and trees line both sides of the fairway, obstructing off-center second shots to the two-tiered green.

Scott Ramsey has widened the undulating fairway and extended it around the left front bunker all the way to the left side of the green. The widened fairway brings into play the effect of balls repelling off the sloping fairway, increasing the difficulty of the hole.

The pin position will determine the flight of your approach shot. The left side of this large green is a bowl protected in front by a deep bunker. The higher, more open right side is protected by two ten-foot bunkers along the right side. In both cases, the bottom of the pin is hidden from the fairway, which makes the second shot deceptively long and causes many shots to fall short.

The flagpole on the first tee was donated by Dr. Allan Brandt, who graduated from the Yale School of Medicine in 1951 and practiced medicine in Milford for forty years. At the base of the flagpole is a bench dedicated to Insoo Hwang. As president of the student body of Seoul University following the Korean War he had served as tour guide for Senator Thomas Dodd, then chairman of the Armed Services Committee. The Senator later sponsored Insoo Hwang's immigration. He taught Judo and Taekwon-do at Yale for more than two decades. Hwang was a strong and enthusiastic golfer. The donor, Higab Moon, was Hwang's childhood friend and later mayor of their hometown, Taegu. They played golf together many times when Moon was an exchange student at Yale. On the left side of the tee is a plaque acknowledging William Beinecke's gift of the first automatic in-ground watering

No. 1 Eli in early fall, 2004

system in 1968. Movie footage taken at the tee box during the first Connecticut Open tournament, held at the course in 1931, shows two large bunkers just before the beginning of the fairway on the right above Greist Pond. They do not appear in the construction or in any subsequent photographs.

No. 2 The Pits
375 yards, 344 yards, 336 yards, par 4

Charles Banks in 1925:

> *This is a natural green heavily bunkered on the left with a rather narrow approach on the right. Much of the green is on natural ground though along the left it has been dramatically built up and features one of the most feared bunkers on the course; a sandpit with a depth in excess of 20 feet. Balls missing this green further left than is bunker will fall into deep oblivion. In general the green can be considered a "Cape setting" jutting out, seemingly into mid-air, rather than out into a body of water.*

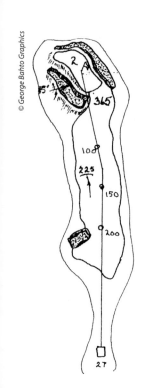

The left-to-right slope of the fairway favors a tee shot that tracks the right side. Scott Ramsay has widened this fairway somewhat, and long drives can run over the hill on the left or repel off the mound on the right. The twin, thirty-foot deep bunkers to the left side of the "cape" green threaten second shots to most pin locations, while a safer approach to the right-side of the green leaves sharply sloping putts towards the deep bunker to the left.

The bench on this tee is dedicated to Dr. Allen "Chet" Chetrick, an avid golfer who always turned in his score to maintain a proper handicap and kept a written record of his daily match play results. An original bunker just over the open watercourse on the left was removed and has not been restored. Removal of trees on the right has revealed an attractive vernal pool. The bunker running the length of the green on the right has been restored. However, the right side of the green, which originally had a high shoulder creating the Redan approach, like the eighth green, was cut down to its present height by Harry Meusel and has not been restored.

Looking from the second fairway towards the Cape green, 2007

Golfers on the second in the 1930s. Note the sight line all the way to the seventh green and eighth tee box. With the recent tree removal, this vista has been restored.

No. 3 Blind
411 yards, 379 yards, 336, par 4

Charles Banks in 1925:

>*The second water hole on the course has a (diagonal) water carry of 118 yards. The hole forces water play as there is no way around. Across the water, the fairway runs parallel to the water on the right and is flanked on the left by high ledges and knolls. The play of the second shot is directly over the saddle between two knolls into a groove between these knolls and a second line of knolls, or directly to the green over the right knoll. The groove leads directly to the green over the right knoll. A long sand trap stretches in front of the first line of knolls. [Editor note: This was removed and not restored.] The green is a double punchbowl with water along the batter on the right and back of it. The fairway undulations of this hole are natural and the hole is most attractive to the eye and furnishes inter-esting play. There is a close and narrow pitch approach to the green on the right but it is very dangerous. [Ed note: This is no longer possible.]*

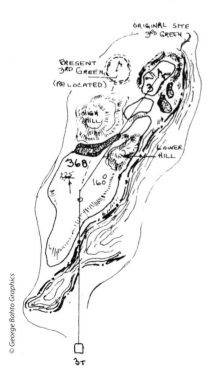

Like the first hole, this par 4 plays from elevated tees over water to an undulating fairway. Unlike the first hole, though, the fairway doglegs right from the back tees. From the regular and forward tees, the fairway is set fully perpendicular to one's drive. The fairway is flanked on the left by high ledges and knolls. Drives that do not reach the beginning of the fairway at the top of the plateau will carom right, and slices will find the water.

Second shots from the fairway are short, but they are blind, played over a ridge to a rather small and right-sloping green.

There have been two significant changes to this hole's design. The original green was a "double punchbowl" that swept around its protective hills and edged over to the pond, as seen in the 1925 construction photo that was taken from the No. 4 tee box, looking back across the third green. Later it was reduced in size so that it is tucked behind the approach hill and is completely hidden from the fairway. Also, in the 1960s, a new "regular" tee box was added to the right of the "long" tee and thirty yards behind the "short" tee. This had been the area that Coach Joe Sullivan used for his short game lessons. The regular tee yardage is unchanged from the original, but the angle is quite different. The evergreens that were planted when the tee was built have been removed. A bench on this tee is dedicated to Bob Tettlebach. He began playing the course in 1937 as a ten-year-old, sneaking on with his older brother Dick. Later he caddied at the course and finally became a member in the 1950s.

The original "double punchbowl" green at No. 3 during construction

No. 4 Road
437 yards, 426 yards, 334 yards, par 4
(women's par is 5/4)

Charles Banks in 1925:

> *The fourth hole has a water carry of 132 yards on the line of play. Play to the left of the line of play lengthens the hole and shortens water carry, while a shot to the right of the line of play not only does the opposite to the left play but also puts the ball in danger from a second arm of the lake, for play to the right of the line of play is upon a peninsula. The approach to the green requires a long, up-hill second shot compelling distance, height and hold due to the nature of the green, which is of the Road Hole of the St. Andrews (Old Course) type, wherein a pot bunker is tangent to the line of play in front of the green and the left approach is lifted. The player may, by using different tees and varying then angle of the dogleg, play the hole with the same distance as that of the original hole.*

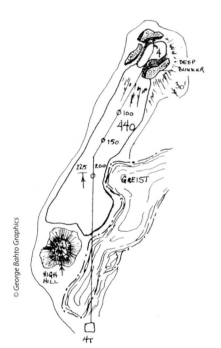

© George Bahto Graphics

Ben Crenshaw said that the fourth is "a perfect use of water as a driving hazard." Indeed, from the regular and back tees, you face your third water carry in four holes. The lake cuts deeply into the fairway in the landing area to catch the longer hitters, who must aim left of center. The second shot with a wood or long iron is to a slightly elevated green protected by a deep pot bunker on the right front side. The thin strip bunkering around the back and left of the green suggests the road at the seventeenth hole of St. Andrews.

Scott Ramsay has recently opened up the hole by removing trees to the right and left and restoring its "line of charm." By that, Ramsay means to charm the player into a line of more risk than he might

1925 construction of the fourth hole. Note that the pond had yet to be excavated and filled in.

normally take in trying to shorten the distance by challenging the pond on the right. His clearing has created a second line of charm in restoring the vista from the tee all the way up to the eighth tee.

Tommy Armour chose this hole as the ninth in his selection of the most difficult holes in the world. George Pepper ranked it as one of the eighteen best (fresh) water holes in the world. A bench dedicated to Sid Kalison sits on the long tee at 4. He joined the course through the Eli Club, after World War II. He was an avid, low handicap golfer until he developed a debilitating neurological illness and had to stop playing in 1990. A highlight of his golfing life was accompanying David Paterson, Bill Beinecke, and others on a golfing holiday to Ireland in 1981. Joe Sullivan's ashes were spread by his twin brothers along the side of the fairway after he died in 1977.

Looking up the fourth fairway, 2008

No. 5 Short
147 yards, 138 yards, 115 yards, Par 3

Charles Banks in 1925:

> The hole is original with Messrs. Macdonald and Raynor and was first put up on National Golf Links of America as hole number six. This is one of the four short holes of the course, i.e. each short hole is designed for a single shot to the green with a particular club. No. 5 is a mashie hole. The tees are slightly above the green level. The green is completely surrounded by sand, making it an island green elevated 12 feet above the level of sand in the bunker. The contours of the green mark a horseshoe around the pin which is placed in the center of the green.

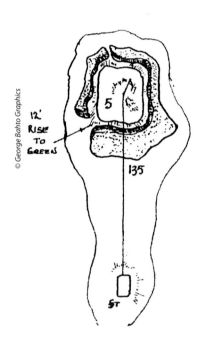

This type of hole was a favorite of C. B. Macdonald and was known as a "horseshoe" or "island." George Bahto notes that Macdonald had been inspired by the fifth hole at Brancaster (now Royal West Norfolk). Bahto also observes that Raynor adapted the design at Yale such that "the plateau height is higher and the rise to the green is more abrupt" than he did elsewhere. As Charles Banks wrote, Raynor intended the mashie (equivalent to a modern 4-iron) to be the appropriate club, and sure enough, just two months after the course opened in 1926, the first hole-in-one was recorded here in June by George Coe Graves II with a mashie. Graves was not only a Yale College freshman but also a golf novice, as Ben Thomson, Yale's first coach at the course, later related in the *American Golfer* (June, 1928):

G. C. Graves, a student, came to me one day and announced that he wanted to take up golf. I fitted him out with a complete set of clubs. Then he suggested that he ought to have some lessons. He never had played at all and he wanted to get a quick start. We set the first lesson for the following Monday. Graves gave me the most serious attention. He was anxious to learn to play well just as quickly as possible. He wasn't at the club on Tuesday. On Wednesday, however, he decided to try his first game. And what do you think he did? At the fifth hole, a short one of 135 yards, he holed his tee-shot!

As with all Yale's par 3's, the fifth hole requires accuracy from the tee. The plateau green is still surrounded by deep bunkers that punish any wayward shots, although narrow wooden stairs up the right side of the green interrupt the bunker line. Installation of under-drainage has raised the

Looking from the fifth tees toward the Island green in the autumn

Peter Heald

bunker sand levels several feet above the original twelve-foot depth.

There are four tee boxes at different elevations, so that nowadays it is ill-advised to play the hole every time with the same club. The line of the hole is perpendicular to the sixth fairway and any wind coming down that fairway will swirl across the fifth green, but it is difficult to detect the strength of the crosswind when standing on the tee. The approach to the green has been widened by removing trees to the right and left, which dramatically emphasizes the view of the green's island elevation. Even so, native grasses obscure the front bunker from most of the tees.

No. 6 Burnside
421 yards, 349 yards, 317 yards, Par 4

Charles Banks in 1925:

> On April 1, 1924, this whole hole was a large swamp impassable except with high top boots. Filling and drainage have brought it to its present pleasant contours. The surface of the present green is six feet above the original land surface. A sharp angle of the swamp remaining on the left cuts in on the left more than half way up the fairway. This angle is guarded by a sand dune. The safest shot is close to this dune and yet clearing it. Safety and distance increase with play to the right. The second shot is a pitch to the green possibly over a broad bunker on the right or avoiding a sand dune on the left. An over-shot is dangerous.

The original notation of this hole was a "natural" design, meaning Raynor designed it to the terrain, not to a Macdonald prototype. The two "sand dunes" mentioned by Banks are gone, but the hole still plays as a dogleg that runs alongside a narrow "burn" (a Scottish word for small stream) on the left.

The burn skirts the woods within which you can see and hear a small waterfall. Above the waterfall, deeper in the woods, remain the fish-hatchery ponds from the old Greist estate.

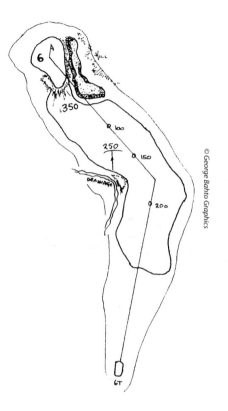

At the elbow of dogleg are the first of the course's three sets of rare dawn redwoods. These are fast-growing trees in the conifer family, also known as meta-sequoias (*Metasequoia glyptostroboides*). They were long thought to be extinct until a small grove was discovered in southwest China in the 1940s and identified by a Chinese paleo-botanist. Samples were collected by an expedition from Harvard's Arnold Arboretum in 1948, and they were distributed to other arboretums and universities for propagation. Several years later, Harry Meusel received a dozen, eighteen-inch seedlings from Dean Mergan of Yale's School of Forestry. Meusel planted three of them along No. 6, one on No. 10, and two on No.18 fairways as part of a 150-yard marker program and placed the remaining six around the maintenance barn. Only the fairway dawn redwoods remain, and what we see today is the mature growth of these distinctive trees.

Sometime between 1926 and 1950, a new long tee was added behind and to the left of the fifth green, which greatly raised the challenge for long hitters trying to shade the dogleg. Recently, Scott Ramsay has cleaned up the burn, improved fairway drainage, and confined the hazard lines on the left of the dogleg to the open watercourse itself (rather than the entire area from burn to woods). This now tempts players even more to risk the "line of charm" across the burn.

Peter Heald

Looking from the fifth green up the sixth fairway as it turns left towards the sixth green in the distance. At the bend are three dawn redwoods.

William W. Kelly

Along the burn of the sixth hole in 2007

The fairway slopes up to the green, and the second shot is deceptively long, often requiring a long iron approach. A tricky forty-yard bunker guards the right side of green, which punishes those who push or slice their approaches. An over-shot is even more dangerous today because the contour of the green was altered in the 1960s. The back of the green was lowered so that an approach shot landing beyond center may not hold.

No. 7 Lane
377 yards, 359 yards, 288, Par 4

Charles Banks in 1925:

> *This hole reminds one of Indian Summer. It is pleasant, inviting and a trifle lazy. The fairway is a natural lane between two ledges on the right, cleared and bare, and tree-covered ledges on the left. The approach to the green is a well rounded knoll and the green winds to the right on the top of the knoll. There is a wide bunker to the right of the green. Play on this hole is better if made to the left hugging the trees so as to get a better entry to the green. In the construction of this hole six feet of solid ledge was taken off the knoll approach and the balance of the fairway was an impass-able swamp.*

This too was a "natural" design, and the fairway treads a narrow lane between a lateral ridge along the right side and long rock ledges along the left. Several decades ago, a new short tee was added here (and at the next hole, No. 8). Both were the gift of Burt Resnik, class of 1934, a member of two national cham-pion teams, and a player here for the rest of his long life. Recent drainage projects have much improved

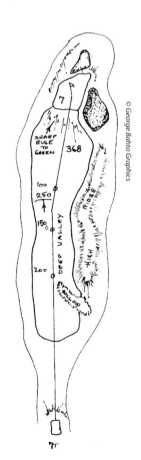

fairway conditions, and tree removal on the left has again exposed the beautiful rock formation of those ledges.

The fairway is level, until it begins to rise steeply eighty yards before the elevated green. This is "Horse Hill," named during construction for one of the work horses that died on the spot and was simply buried there. Scott Ramsay has extended the fairway cut all the way up the hill to the green — and extended the green's front edge

Final shaping of the seventh fairway and green in 1925

several feet down the hill, giving a new, frightening meaning to the term "false front"! The tri-level green is treacherously pitched from back to front, and any pin location will sorely test one's putting.

We recommend a walk of more than a mile on the old construction service road. This begins in front of the new short tee, passes the Bird Sanctuary, the fish hatching ponds of Greist, and then continues through forest that has not been disturbed for at least 100 years, and ends behind

Working the horses on Horse Hill, 1925

the long tee on No. 15. You could also take a right turn just past the Bird Sanctuary and go up to the highest point behind the seventh green to the Wilbur Cross Parkway where the original irrigation water tower was located. This trail ends at Fountain Street.

No. 8 Cape
406 yards, 383 yards, 328 yards, Par 4

Charles Banks in 1925:

> The first shot of this hole is 180 yards to a saddle crossing the fairway. A roll up or carry of the knoll gives a roll down the other side of the saddle into a broad level basin making 220 yards not difficult. The basin is the playing area for the second shot. The second shot should be a kick in front of the front right corner of the green. The green combines characteristics of both the Cape and the Redan.

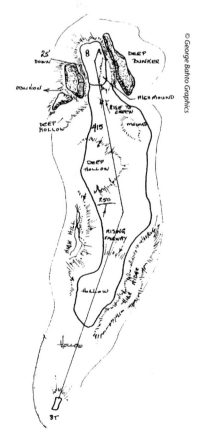

© George Bahto Graphics

The drive for this hole is from the highest-elevation tees on the course, offering beautiful sight lines but yielding no view of the fairway itself, which must be reached by carrying a saddle. The hole is a slight dogleg to the left (and recent brush-clearing now offers a view of the green from the tee), tempting players to aim for that side of the fairway, but the sharp, side slope all along the left side will penalize any ball that misses the fairway. The fairway itself is, as Banks found it, a "broad level basin," but the second shot, also blind, requires precise placement to a narrow, but exceedingly long green, which is canted right-to-left and back-to-front.

Scott Ramsay has added to the green at its front, increasing total size from 14,000 to 19,000 square feet, and he has expanded the 'kick' space before the green, offering players even more options for approach. Nonetheless, the green remains one of the most difficult on the whole

Approaching the eighth green, circa 1926

course, combining the most challenging features of a Cape and a Redan. As an extreme Cape, it stands above thirty-foot deep bunkers to the left and the right. As an exaggerated Redan, it is mounded eight feet higher on its right side, allowing skilled players to play for strategic rolls but threatening other shots with accelerating runs across the green to the left side and below.

Approaching to the eighth green today

No. 9 Biarritz
213 yards, 196 yards, 166/146 yards, Par 3

Charles Banks in 1925:

> This hole has its original on the Biarritz course at the
> famous watering hole in France of the same name …. There
> is a 163 yard carry from the back tee. The green proper is
> behind a deep trench in the approach. The approach is about
> the same size as the green itself
> and is bunkered heavily on both
> right and left with water jutting
> in on the right front. The
> fairway is the lake …. The green
> is heavily battered at the back
> and right and the whole
> psychology of the hole is to let
> out to the limit …. Correct play
> for this green is to carry to the
> near edge of the groove or trench
> and come up on the green with a
> roll. The disappearance and
> reappearance of the ball in the
> groove adds to the interest of the
> play.

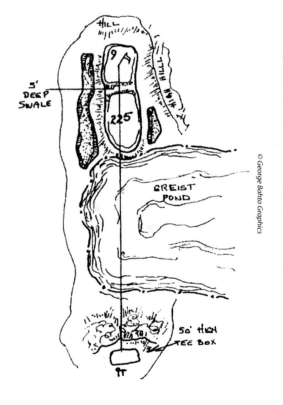

© George Bahto Graphics

Playing again from an
elevated tee, the golfer faces
another water carry to an enormous two-tiered green, some
sixty-four yards deep. What is
most interesting in Banks's 1925 description is that originally
the "green proper" was only beyond the deep "groove," and he
considered the flat landing after the water and before the
groove to be an "approach" area. It has now been incorporated

Yale Athletics Archives

Constructing Yale's ninth hole in 1925

as the front half of the green, protected on right and left by bunkers.

Club selection and shot height depend entirely on pin location. When the pin is in the front, you need a high soft shot to hold the front part of the green, which is fairly level. When the pin is in the back, you can hit a lower trajectory that will land in the front and run through the swale up on to the back green. Although that part of the green is angled right to left, you are still often left with a very fast side hill putt.

The original short tees were set with the regular tees on the high ground. Only later were two forward tee boxes created near the base of the tee and at the front edge of Greist Pond. Ramsay's recent removal of trees behind the tee as well as behind and to the right and left of the green has greatly improved turf conditions in both areas.

This hole is dedicated to Widdy Neale, whose name is also honored as the "nineteenth" hole in the Clubhouse. On the regular tee is a bench dedicated to Dr. Hugh Dwyer, who played on the same high school golf team as Tom Watson's father in Kansas City. He graduated from Northwestern School of Medicine and did his residency at Yale, later working as a physician assigned to care for atomic scientists

Larry Lambrecht

The ninth green

in World War II at Oak Ridge, Los Alamos, and Hanford. Dwyer returned to New Haven and was an avid member of the course, always walking and carrying a single-digit handicap. Late in his life, his left arm was amputated to remove a cancer, but he continued to play and continued to carry his bag; his handicap rose only to twelve! As far as we know, he is the only one-armed golfer ever to have a hole-in-one on the ninth hole, which he achieved in an Eli Club tournament in 1985. As he requested, Dr. Dwyer's ashes were spread on the course.

No. 10 Carries
396 yards, 360 yards, 305/235 yards, Par 4

Charles Banks in 1925:

> Another fine hole is the 10th, a par 4 high-lighted by the most severely undulating putting surface at Yale, a complex and slippery green set high on a hillside terrace that severely punishes careless placement from the fairway approach. Regardless of the pin's position on the rolling swaying green, even the shortest putts have an alarming tendency to creep by the hole and wander away. The hole bears a strong resemblance to the famous 9th at Shinnecock. The green is highly undulating so as to furnish a sure landing when a ball reaches it. The play for this hole is to get as much distance on the first plateau as possible in order to make the second shot reach the green .... The second shot requires both height and distance.

A blind, uphill tee shot must carry a ridge to an elevated saddle, which then drops down to a lower flat fairway. Beyond the landing area, about seventy-five yards in front of the green, is

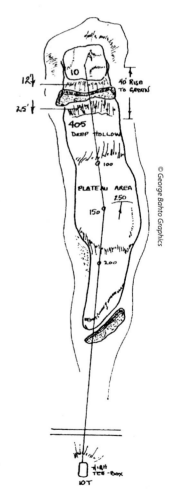

© George Bahto Graphics

William W. Kelly

a sharp rise to shallow bunkers (the "aprons" of the hole's original design name) that front a highly undulating green that sits another twelve feet above the bunkers. Because they play uphill severely, second shots are blind as well. The green itself is two-tiered and angled right to left so that any pin placements center and left can easily funnel putts past the hole and into the lower tier.

Dawn Redwood on the right side of the tenth fairway

On the right side of the lower fairway plateau is the second place-ment of the dawn redwood saplings, of which a single tree remains, now sixty-feet tall. The photo to the left features this dawn redwood in the foreground, with a view through the eighteenth fairway to the dawn

Michael Marsland

Looking back from the tenth green, 2007

redwood on that hole. Originally there were two large bunkers on the hill leading up to the beginning of the fairway, 170 yards from the long tee. These were removed before 1950. Two new short tees were added, one before that area and one just beyond it, about twenty years ago. Some of the trees to the left and behind the green are being removed.

No. 11 Valley
379 yards, 340 yards, 324 yards, Par 4

Charles Banks in 1925:

> As contrasted with number ten which is practically all up hill, number 11 is practically all down hill. The tee is high above the green and the fairway immediately in front. From the tee, Long Island and the Sound are readily visible when not covered by fog. The play to this hole is to reach the second knoll and catch a roll over the far shoulder when there is an easy pitch to the green. The green is a reversed Redan and the hole is a two shot Redan. Play to the left of the line of play direct to the green gives a little better facing to the green for the kick-in play to which the green is best adapted. The green is backed on the left by a long bunker and has a long bunker on the right. The hole is essentially a drive and a pitch hole.

Most Redan holes are par-3s, which is why Banks specified this par-4 as a two-shot Redan. And the classic Redan green is a banked curve from front right to back left, but here the green is curved from left to right. The hole plays all downhill, from the high tees looking down a fairway below that is bisected by a low saddle. A

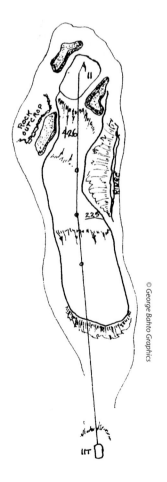

© George Bahto Graphics

Peter Heald

Looking down the eleventh fairway

good drive will clear the saddle and feed into the landing area in front of the green. Long hitters will need to avoid the large bunker on the side slope to the left of the fairway, which is backed by a rock face.

Scott Ramsay removed tree growth behind the green, which returned the original look of the hole and also makes it more difficult to judge the distance of one's second shot. He extended the already long green even further in the front, encouraging running approach shots. The green itself is relatively level, but it still requires a delicate approach because it falls away subtly to the right side bunker and to the back.

The bench on this tee was a gift of Fritz Meusel, Harry Meusel's brother. Fritz is the same age as the course, and he has been playing it since 1971. He selected this spot so that those who had made the strenuous walk from the ninth green to the tenth tee and then over the hills and up to the tenth green and eleventh tee would have a place to rest. This is the hole on which Fritz has had two eagles (so far)!

In 1995 Dick Tettelbach's family spread his ashes near the left fairway bunker and along the trail behind the ledge that leads to the home of Dick's golfing friend, Arnie Whitten. The plantings behind the bunker reminded him of places that he liked to go hiking in western Massachusetts and Vermont.

Tettelbach played left field on the Yale baseball team, including two years as a teammate of George H.W. Bush. He captained the 1950 squad and went on to spend five years in the New York Yankees' minor league organization. He played two games for the Yankees in 1955 before he was traded to the Washington Senators. On opening day in 1956, against the Yankees, and with President Eisenhower in the stands, he hit his only major league home run off ace Don Larsen. (David Paterson relates that as a young Scottish golf professional, new to the States, the very first baseball game he ever saw was the perfect game that Don Larsen threw in the World Series later in 1956. He admits that he couldn't figure out what everyone was so excited about!) Because of his friendship with Whitey Herzog from their minor league days, Tettlebach was invited to spring training with the St Louis Cardinals for several years while Whitey was the manager. Tettlebach returned to Connecticut and was very active in the Connecticut State Golf Association as a tournament official,

Michael Marsland

Looking back from the eleventh green

course rater, and president. The CSGA now awards the Tettelbach Award to its "Amateur of the Year." For forty years, he
was the president and the guiding spirit of the Eli Club at the
Yale course. He was six times the Yale Club champion. In 2006,
he was inducted into the Connecticut Golf Hall of Fame.

No. 12 Alps
400 yards, 350 yards, 318 yards, Par 4

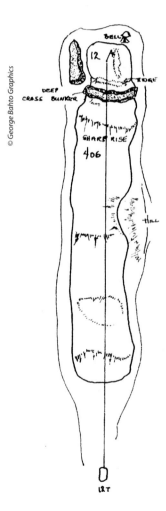

Charles Banks in 1925:

*This hole is intended in its original form to
give the player the feeling of playing up on the
side of a mountain to a hidden pocket. From the
back tee of this hole the ledge at the back of the
green is visible in outline above the elevation in
the front of the green. Men on the green are
entirely out of view. From the position of the
second shot only the mound in front of the green
is visible. The second shot is to play over the
mound in front of the green. A roll up and over
this mound is punished by a bunker on the left
side and is highly undulated. For the first shot a
carry of 176 yards from the back of the tee catches
the near side of the knoll for a roll over to the level
playing ground for the second shot.*

As the golfer realizes by now, Macdonald
and Raynor respected the complex topography
of the Greist estate and left many of the fairways undulated by saddles, knolls, and swales.
This hole is yet another example, and, as its
name suggests, it is intended to give the feeling
of playing up the side of a mountain to a hidden
pocket.

© George Bahto Graphics

The view of the 12th fairway from in front of the tee

A semi-blind tee shot is played straight over a saddle of fescue to the fairway landing area beyond. This fairway rises gently and then more steeply, towards a green that lies beyond a high cross ridge that hides a bunker between it and the green itself. The green is wider than it is deep, and it is split-level, bisected front to back such that the left side is higher than the right side.

Nowhere has Scott Ramsay's restoration been more dramatic. Tree removal around the long tee and on both sides of the knoll has returned the view from the tees to the first shot landing area to that seen in early photographs. The fairway has been extended all the way up and over the cross-ridge. The wide lateral bunker in front of the green has been restored to the original, and trees and brush behind the green have been removed to fit the Banks description from the tee to green.

Michael Marsland

Looking back across the green of No. 12 "Alps"

Behind the green is a bell to be rung when the green is cleared. It was a gift of Dr. Irving Glassman, who practiced radiology for forty years. He began playing the Yale course in 1985, when he was associated with the Yale Health Services. Even now, in his mid-eighties, he is still playing three days a week.

No.13 Redan
212 yards, 196 yards, 189 yards, Par 3

Charles Banks in 1925:

> *The third water hole is the regular Redan or one shot hole for the cleek* [Ed.: the equivalent of today's 1-iron or 4-wood]. *The original hole is on the North Berwick course in Scotland. In levels and undulations this green closely resembles the original but has a different setting. The line of play cuts the green diagonally from front to back right corner. The green slopes down to the back. The pin set at the back left corner for championship play. The approach to the green rises to the green proper whence the green slopes away to the back with the front right corner the highest point on the green. From the above it is evident that the play for the green is to catch the approach a little above and beyond its center for a kick in or carom off the right corner and a curving roll across the green to the pin at the back left corner. When properly executed the play of this green is one of the most pleasing and interesting plays in golf. The tee for this hole is 48 feet above the surface of the water, partially crossing the*

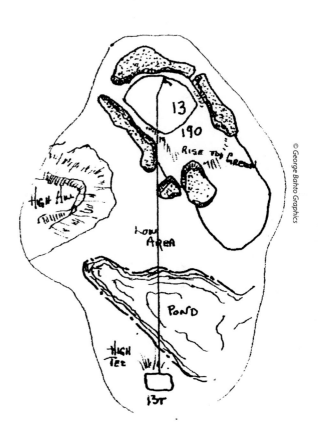

Michael Marsland

No. 13 Redan in 2007

fairway. Directly in front of the approach a broad bunker runs across the fairway necessitating a carry of 150 yards to safety. The fairway is flanked on either side by high knolls so that a straight shooting and a 150-yard carry are the compelling influence of the hole. The green is bunkered along the right and left sides making short cuts dangerous.

Banks's original prose well describes the perils of this long par-three. The green itself remains true to its North Berwick model, sloping sharply to the left from its highest point at the back right corner. Here at Yale, however, the tee box is set high above the hole, offering a stunning view that rises from a small pond at the base of the tee box to the green itself, wrapped by a tree line and protected on four sides by bunkers. Two bunkers were restored behind the green to regain this "surround" effect.

The challenge of the tee shot here is to drop it precisely onto the back right corner of the green to take advantage of the Redan roll. Scott Ramsay has extended the green to create another false front that rejects short approach shots.

Looking back from the green to the tee, with no leaves on the trees, one can appreciate the hand work it took to build the rock retaining wall that supports the tee. The laurels on the hillside in front of the tee were transplanted from behind the ninth hole. In the 1950s, Harry Meusel suspended his workers from ropes to do these plantings. Meusel developed a passion for Japanese garden design, taking seminars at Yale, and traveling to Japan to study famous gardens. This inspired him to design and build a small Japanese-style garden next to the pond below the tee, which is now being restored.

On the tee itself are two memorials. The bench "Fore Steve" is in memory of Steve LaMantia, who played in the Beinecke Tournament with Chris Moran '86, Ted Moran '86, and Joe Glancy on September 9, 2001. Two days later, at age

William W. Kelly

"Fore — Steve": Memorial bench at the thirteenth tee

thirty-eight, he perished at the World Trade Center. Chris Moran says that the bench "was placed at the top of the thirteenth tee as an informal acknowledgement of some golf magic that happened at No. 13 that Sunday." The other bronze plate is mounted on a rock at the beginning of the cart path and commemorates the gift of the 150-yard evergreen markers that were planted in the 1960s by the Wareck family.

No.14 Knoll
365 Yards, 343 Yards, 331 Yards, Par 4

Charles Banks in 1925:

> *Number 14 offers in its first shot three different attacks on the playing ground for the second shot. The first of these from the back tee plays for a kick in to the right from a knoll on the left side of the fairway at the angle of the dogleg with a consequent roll to low ground in front of the green. The shot from the regular tee offers the same shot with a distance to the target of 37 yards less, or if desired, a straight shot to the playing ground over the trees. The shot from the short tee is a straightaway down the fairway with the green in sight all the way. All of these shots lead to the same playing ground for the second shot. The second shot is a lift and hold. The green is elevated on all sides and slopes to the left. There is a large bunker at the back.*

This is a deceptively compact par-four, made challenging by its tilts, angles, and uneven lies. The most prominent feature in the sight line from the tees is the knoll that defines the left side of the fairway as it sweeps around a bend from left to right. The knoll begins a low lateral ridge that allows the player to bank drives off the left side of the fairway forward and towards the green, although misses to the left will push errant balls towards the woods. A well-shaped drive — or bold drive that cuts the near corner to the right — will find itself below an elevated green that slopes steeply away on all sides. The original bunker in back has been replaced with a greater hazard, a

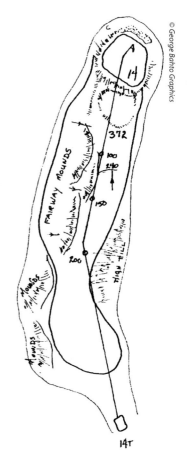

swamp played as a lateral hazard. The effects of Scott Ramsay's tree-clearing are seen here, too, to dramatic effect. Their removal at the fairway bend opens up a view of the green, and cutting back the trees to the right of the green further enhances the dogleg effect as well as improving the health of the green.

It is the fairway knoll that gives the hole its name, and appropriately, although coincidentally, it is based originally on the fourth hole at Scotscraig Golf Course, the course where the young Robert Pryde learned his golfing craft in the 1880s before emigrating to New Haven. As George Bahto noted, Macdonald and Raynor used this design at their famous Piping Rock and Lido courses before applying it here. As noted earlier, the memory of Harry Meusel is also present in the form of the forest elf carved by his daughter and still standing in the woods to the right of the dogleg.

The fourteenth hole (Knoll)

Looking back from the fifteenth tees towards the fourteenth green

No.15 Eden
190 Yards, 165 Yards, 126 Yards, Par 3

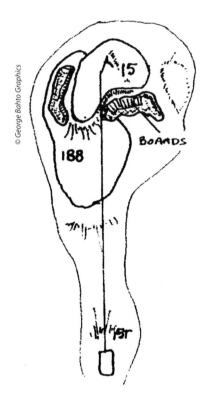

Charles Banks in 1925:

This is the Eden hole which has its original on the St. Andrews course in Scotland. This is the fourth and last of the short holes and is a one shot with the iron. The regular tee gives the customary distance for the iron (175 yards). In its original setting this green has the river Eden flowing along the back. From the tee it appears that the river touches the back of the green but in reality the river is beyond the bunker which crossed the back of the green. The bunkers on the right and left of this green are named Strath Bunker on the right and the Shelley Bunker on the left. This green has a different setting. In the case of the short holes the fairway of the fairgreen is missing and the intervening space is rough. From all holes the rough extends some 129 yards from tee before the smooth fairgreen begins.

Looking up at the fifteenth green in early spring, 2008

In removing trees that had crept into the left side of the length of the hole, Scott Ramsay has opened up the original sight line from the tees. Restoration of the oddly-shaped Strath Bunker and elimination of the railroad ties that had been added to its face in the 1960s have much improved the bunker's appearance and playability. Ramsay has also extended the front lip of the green and created an apron of fairway below. This allows more creative run-up shots, but putts from above any front pin locations can now quickly slide off the front edge of the green. Better management of the fescue grasses that sweep behind the green accentuates their evocation of the flowing river Eden.

No. 16 Lang
553 Yards, 474 Yards, 435 Yards, Par 5

Charles Banks in 1925:

> *Number sixteen is a rather long rolling fairway leading to a broad level green. The hole should be found somewhat of a let-down from the preceding and following holes of the second nine. The second shot of this hole is the critical one and should bring the ball up from an easy pitch to the green. The green is hidden from the tees and a shot for a narrow transverse saddle in the fairway should open up the hole for the second and third.*

Since 1926, three tee boxes have been added to the original tee, which is now the short, and the hole plays as a par 5 from all tees. At 553 yards, the new long tee is 210 yards to the fairway, making this a real par 5, even for the long hitters. The woods along both sides of the straight line to the hole reward straight play. However, the undulations of the first half of the fairway that leads to a narrow saddle will often create awkward stances that add a degree of difficulty to the second shot.

The second half of the fairway opens up and flattens out for the approach. Seth Raynor's 1925

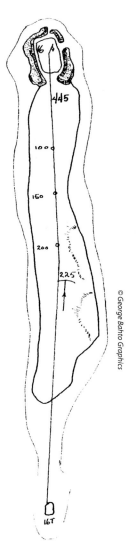

© George Bahto Graphics

schematic plan showed water on the left front of this green. Now, however, shallow bunkers surround the long green, which slopes back left to front center and front right. Roger Rulewich restored the right-side bunker and extended it partially around the front of the green. Previously, a shot could kick off the higher right side of the fairway and run up on the green. The bunker now pinches the front collar and heightens the risk in trying for the green in two shots.

Michael Marsland

The sixteenth in 2008

No. 17 Nose
437 Yards, 395 Yards, 390/242 Yards, Par 4

Charles Banks in 1925:

> *The play from the tee is over the last of the six water fairways at the far side of which is a lift of 20 feet from the water's surface. The carry to the top of the lift opens up the hole. The ground from the edge of the left slopes down to the green at a good angle so that a good roll may be expected. The green is composed of three plateaus with an opening at the back between two of them and upon the low one. The approach to the green on the left is guarded by a mound flanked with bunkers, one on the left, one at the right, both visible from the playing ground fro the second shot and a third behind the knoll next to the green which is hidden from the player making the second shot. This hazard is known as the Principal's Nose and originates on the St. Andrews course. The approach on the right is smooth but not broad and travel that way may present a putting hazard unless the pin is on the low plateau.*

Originally, all three tees were found where the present long tees are located, but subsequently, the regular tees were moved to the front edge of the pond, and the new short tees were built at the top of the hill tucked into the right corner. Banks noted a "lift of 20 feet above the water's surface" across the pond from the regular and long tees, but he neglected to warn that this lift was actually an exposed rock ledge that rejected low drives back into the swamp. During the

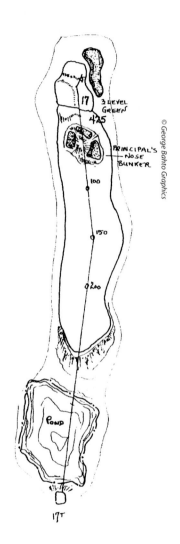

© *George Bahto Graphics*

The drive from the regular tees requires elevation to carry the "lift."

drought of 1965, the swamp was converted into a pond and the ledge became a steep hillside by pushing the swamp muck up against the ledge.

Nonetheless, the drive across the pond requires height and distance to clear the top of the hill and gain the fairway, which then slopes gently down towards the green. Scott Ramsay has cut back the native grasses on either side to widen the fairway in its landing area, but drives to the left and right can find rough, fescue, and the woods. The three bunkers around the "Principal's Nose" have all been restored, as well as the bunker along the entire right side of the green. Ramsay has extended the fairway around the Principal's Nose and is keeping the grass on the Nose cut short.

The green itself is typically expansive and tiered both to the left and in the back right, requiring an accurate approach shot to avoid a treacherous putt. In 2006, when Rees Jones

Michael Marsland

came to tour the course for the first time in several years, this was the green he most wanted to see again, to determine if it was as difficult as he remembered. (It was!)

Looking down the seventeenth fairway with the Principal's Nose guarding the approach to the green

No.18 Home
621 Yards, 542 Yards, 480 Yards, Par 5

Charles Banks in 1925:

> *This is a long fellow. To relieve the tedium of the drag through a long hole where distance is the only commendation, this hole has been broken up into three distinct parts. The first shot should carry over a shoulder at the right and at the angle of the dogleg. By carry the brow of this shoulder and making a roll over, the ball is brought to a smooth area of playing ground for the second. The second play to the top of*

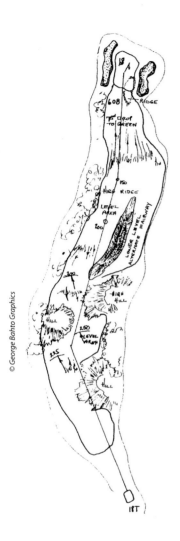

the hill which has been leveled off and cut down so as to make the green visible from the second play area. The shot is to the green on the third. Should the player desire to avoid the hill he may play around the right with a penalty of increased distance. The two playing grounds for the second and third shots are practically two greens to shoot at but of twice or three times the area of ordinary putting greens.

Getting "home" is a severe test of blind shots, multiple options, and rugged topography. It is indeed a "natural" design and unique challenge!

Scott Ramsay notes about his recent work, "On number eighteen can be seen the most dramatic results of tree removal and the reduction of penal native grass. Now there are wide-open areas for both the first and second shots and multiple options for club selection and direction of play." From the back tees, a long drive is needed over the shoulder of first hill to the lower fairway, tucked beyond the hill. The left edge of the fairway is marked by the third set of rare dawn redwoods. You can play the second shot to the top of an intimidating fairway plateau hill, from which you will have an equally steep downhill approach to the green. Or you can play the second shot to the right, aiming for the lower fairway channel. Ramsay is now keeping the grass on the side of the hill cut short so that second shots that find the hill will not settle but roll on to the lower fairway. The fairway itself has been widened to the right-side tree line, but all shots from this lower landing area are blind shots to the green.

The fescued shoulder of a low hill hides the landing area for drives from the eighteenth-hole tees.

The final slope

The final approach to reach "home": construction in 1925

There is a lateral brook near the eighteenth green on the right side of fairway. A five-foot deep bunker running the length of its left side and a smaller bunker on the right side penalize errant approaches. The green itself is exceptionally large, testing the golfer to the final putt.

The final approach to reach "home" in 2007

Men's and Women's Golf Team Records and Honors 1897-2009

Team Records and Honors, 1897-2009

NATIONAL TITLES (21): 1897, 1898 (Fall), 1902 (Spring), 1905, 1906, 1907, 1908, 1909, 1910, 1911, 1912, 1913, 1915, 1924, 1925, 1926, 1931, 1932, 1933, 1936, 1943 (Note: Yale leads all colleges in its title total. The University of Houston is second with sixteen titles.)

MEN'S EIGA CHAMPIONSHIPS (20): 1931, 1932, 1933, 1934, 1935, 1936, 1937, 1938, 1942, 1949, 1951, 1953, 1954, 1956, 1958, 1959, 1962, 1965, 1971

MEN'S IVY LEAGUE CHAMPIONSHIPS (13): 1957, 1958, 1959, 1962, 1966, 1984, 1985, 1988, 1990, 1991, 1996, 1997, 2003

WOMEN'S EIGA CHAMPIONSHIPS (6): 1984, 1985, 1988, 1990, 1991, 1996

WOMEN'S IVY LEAGUE CHAMPIONSHIPS (6): 1997, 1998, 2000, 2003, 2005, 2006

MEN'S ALL-AMERICANS: 1960 (Second Team) — Ted Weiss; 1963 (Third Team) — Daniel Hogan; 1965 (Honorable Mention) — Ned Snyder; 1974 (HM) — Bob Goodyear; 1976 (HM), 1977 (Third Team), 1978 (Third Team) — Peter Teravainen; 1980 (HM) — Trip Long; 1984 (Third Team) — Bill Huddleston

MEN'S USGA NATIONAL INTERCOLLEGIATE INDIVIDUAL CHAMPIONS: 1898 (Spring) John Reid, Jr.; 1902 (Spring) — Charles Hitchcock, Jr.; 1905 — Robert Abbott; 1906 — W. E. Crow, Jr.; 1907 — Ellis Knowles; 1910 — Robert Hunter; 1911 — George Stanley; 1915 — Francis Blossom; 1920 — Jess Sweetser; 1923, 1924 — Dexter Cummings; 1929 — Tom Aycock
MEN'S IVY LEAGUE INDIVIDUAL CHAMPIONS: 1977, 1978 — Peter Teravainen; 1984 — Jim Goff; 1985 — Bill Huddleston; 1988 — Chip Arndt; 1990, 1991, 1992 — Bob Heintz; 1996 — Ken Rizvi; 1999 — Chris Eckerle; 2001 — Louis Aurelio
WOMEN'S IVY LEAGUE INDIVIDUAL CHAMPIONS: 1998 — Natalie Wong; 2000 — Sarah Seo; 2005 — Cindy Shin

Men's Varsity Golf Captains, 1897-2009

1897	TERRY, Roderick, Jr.	1912	GARDNER, Robert A.
1898	TERRY, Roderick, Jr.	1913	STANLEY, George C.
1899	Unknown	1914	WHEELER, Nathaniel
1900	HAVEMEYER, Frederick C.	1915	GARDNER, William H., 2nd
1901	ROBERTSON, T. Markoe	1916	MUDGE, Dudley H.
1902	HITCHCOCK, Charles, Jr.	1917	BALCH, DeWitt W.
1903	CAMPBELL, Nelson S.	1918	BALCH, DeWitt W.
1904	REID, Archibald M.	1919	DAVIS, Thomas B.
1905	SMITH, Bruce D.	1920	SCOTT, Sidney
1906	CLOW, William E.	1921	SCOTT, Sidney
1907	ABBOTT, Robert	1922	BUFFINGTON, Azariah T.
1908	VAN VLECK, Charles E.	1923	LOVELL, Nathaniel T.
1909	Unknown	1924	BOWLES, Chester B.
1910	MERRIMAN, Buckingham P.	1925	CUMMINGS, Dexter
1911	MOSSER, Karl E.	1926	WATTLES, Frank E., Jr.

1927	HAVILAND, Paul	1961	WALKER, J. Frost
1928	LANMAN, William K.	1962	LOBSTEIN, Philip
1929	FORREST, Marshall W.	1963	MOZELESKI, Stuart
1930	FORREST, Marshall W.	1964	HOUT, Thomas
1931	SWOOPE, Walter M.	1965	HOGAN, Daniel
1932	ENGLAND, Dan	1966	SNYDER, Edward
1933	PARKER, John E., Jr.	1967	RYDELL, John R., 2nd
1934	TRANSUE, Oliver M.	1968	ROGERS, Jim
1935	TOWN, Frederick B.	1969	POLACKWICH, Robert
1936	ESHELMAN, Herbert R.	1970	WILLNER, Hank
1937	MUNSON, C. Sherwood	1971	COLLIER, Paul
1938	JAMISON, Paul B., Jr.	1972	SANDERSON, Chase
1939	MERRITT, Haines R.	1973	ROBBINS, Todd
1940	MEISTER, Edward, Jr.	1974	GOODYEAR, Robert
1941	SCOTT, J. Virgil, Jr.	1975	SARGENT, Mark
1942	GRAVELY, Edmund K.	1976	MARTINSON, Ross
1943	WILLIAMS, Arthur C. "Ace"	1977	THON, Rich
1944	No competition	1978	TERAVAINEN, Peter
1945	No competition	1979	LYSTAD, Scott
1946	NEITHAMER, Calvin D.	1980	WARNER, Jim
1947	RAMSEY, George K.	1981	WARNER, Jim
1948	BOOE, William A.	1982	CONNELLY, John
1949	BATES Guy C.	1983	WARD, Seth
1950	BIRDSTON, Paul J.	1984	BORAH, Tom
1951	HEALEY, James	1985	HUDDLESTON, Bill
1952	RODEN, Lincoln	1986	GOFF, Jim
1953	KILREA, Walter	1987	SEVERTSON, Mark
1954	WISLAR, George H.	1988	LORENZE, Mark
1955	FEHR, Gerald	1989	SHANLEY, Justin
1956	VARE, Edwin C.	1990	ARNDT, Chip
1957	NISSELSON, Peter	1991	STRACKS, John
1958	DOLP, Franz	1992	HEINTZ, Bob
1959	SUISMAN, John	1993	WARGO, Brad
1960	WEISS, Theodore	1994	WARGO, Brad

1995	KOHANSKY, Gregg	2003	WILLIAMS, Neel
1996	PIERCE, Brian	2004	LEVY, Ben
1997	RIZVI, Nader	2005	GRAY, Steve
1998	BRINKER, Scott	2006	REISSMAN, Rick
1999	BENEROFE, Gary	2007	MATZA, Mark
2000	SCHUMACHER, Peter	2008	DENEBERG, Andrew
2001	AURIELO, Louis	2009	MOORE, Colby
2002	ECKERLE, Chris		

Women's Varsity Team Captains, 1981-2009

1981	FRANCUS, Andrea	1996	WONG, Natalie
1982	FRANCUS, Andrea	1997	WONG, Natalie
1983	CAVANAGH, Susan	1998	WONG, Natalie
1984	CAVANAGH, Susan	1999	FISHER, Kate
1985	JINKINS, Sue	2000	JOHNSON, Emily
1986	BARTLETT, Mary	2001	SEO, Sarah
1987	LANE, Mary	2002	SEO, Sarah
1988	CASEY, Gillian	2003	DAVIS, Jordanna
1989	SPOLYAR, Mary	2004	WEI, Stephanie
1990	TOTH, Cynthia	2005	RESSLER, Lauren
1991	PATTERSON, Ashley	2006	ROMERO, January
1992	DAMGARD, Julie	2007	SHIN, Cindy
1993	GILL, Wendy	2008	BROPHY, Ellen
1994	LEE, J. Mi	2009	SPACKEY, Natasha
1995	VOTAVA, Julie		

Varsity Golf Letter Recipients, Men, 1911-2008

Note: Although intercollegiate golf teams date from 1896, varsity golfers were not awarded letters in the sport until 1911. Even then, a distinction was drawn between a major "Y" for football, crew, basketball, baseball, track and field, and a minor "Y," which was awarded to varsity golf and tennis players. This distinction continued until 1950. More recently, a minor "Y" was awarded to team members who did not play in a minimum number of major tournaments.The asterisk below denotes a minor "Y." The "S" following class year refers to Sheffield Science School, the science and engineering school at Yale from 1847 to 1956.

A

ALBAN, Blake M. '95	1992, 93, 94
ALLEN, Frederick F. '38	1935*, 38*
ALLEN, George D. '59	1959 (Mgr)
AMORY, E. Horton, Jr. '37s	1937*
ARMSTRONG, Dwight L. '17	1916*, 17*
ARNDT, Willis C. '90	1988, 89, 90
ARONSTEIN, Michael C. '74	1973, 74
AURELIO, Louis '01	1998, 99, 00
AYCOCK, Thomas J., Jr. '31s	1929, 29*, 31

B

BADER, Lawrence N. '63	1961, 62, 63
BADHAM, William T. '17s	1916*
BALCH, DeWitt '18	1916*
BANNEROT, F. '29S	1929*
BARDWELL, Robert D., Jr. '42	1942*
BARNES, Bert D. '69	1967, 68, 69 (Mgr)
BARTON, Robert K. '54	1952, 53
BATES, Guy C. '49e	1947*, 48*, 49
BATES, R. Dennis '63	1963 (Mgr)
BAXTER, Charles McG. '14	1914*
BEACH, Richard E. '49	1948*
BECKJORD, Walter E. '44s	1942* (2)
BENEROFE, Gary M. '99	1996, 97, 98, 99

BERCOVICH, David '99	1996, 97, 98, 99
BISCOE, Howard M. '24	1924
BISHOP, Julian T. '14	1913*, 14*
BLACKBURN, William W., 2nd '41s	1941*
BLANCHARD, J. Alden '21s	1921*
BLOSSOM, Francis R. '17	1915*, 16*, 17*
BOHN, Nathan D. '99	1997, 98, 99
BOOE, William A. '49	1947*, 48*, 49
BORAH, Thomas M. '85	1982, 83, 84, 85
BORDERS, Melville W. '19	1919*
BORRUD, Gabriel '06	2003, 04, 06
BORSODI, F. '39s	1937*, 38*, 39*
BOTT, Tazewell M. '42	1942*
BOWLES, Charles A. '13s	1913*
BOWLES, Chester B. '24s	1924
BOYLE, Alexander R.M., Jr. '59	1958, 59
BRANDOW, John M. '75	1973, 74
BREDIN, Lewis L. '16	1915*, 16*
BRIDSTON, Paul J. '50	1948*, 49*, 50
BRINKER, Scott M. '99	1996, 97, 98, 99
BROCKNER, Eddie '01	1998, 99, 00
BROKAW, John I. '52	1952 (Mgr)
BROWN, Gordon C. '41	1940*
BROWN, J. Stuart, 3rd '51e	1949*, 50*, 51
BUFFINTON, Azariah T. '22	1921*

BURKE, B. James '38s	1938*	DAVENPORT, Huntley G. '60	1960 (Mgr)
BURNHAM, S.W. '??	1919* (Mgr)	DAVIS, Thomas B. '19	1917*, 19*
BUSH, James S. '22	1921*	DeLUDE, Anthony M. '57	1956, 57
BUSH, Prescott S. '17	1915*	DEMMON, Roy E. '48	1945, 46*, 48*
BUTTERWORTH, Guy A. '61	1961 (Mgr)	DENENBERG, Andrew '08	2005, 06, 07, 08
		de SWAAN, Jean Christophe '93	1990*, 91, 92, 93

C

		DeWALT, Frederic B. '47n	1945, 46*
CALLAN, Edward F., Jr. '40	1939*, 40*	DeWITT, William O. '90	1988, 89, 90
CARR, Donald J. '37	1937*	DHAWAN, Dashrath '03	2000*
CARROLL, John K. '77	1976	DOLP, Franz '58	1956, 57, 58
CARROLL, Thomas E. '50	1950* (Mgr)	DONNELLY, Stan D., Jr. '46m	1945, 46*
CHATFIELD-TAYLOR, Wayne '16	1915*	DONNELLY, William A., Jr. '68	1967
CHEPIGA, Geoffrey '02	2000*	DOW, F. Lawrence '28	1928*
CHILD, William K. '27s	1927*	DOYLE, Matthew N. '77	1974
CLARK, LeRoy, Jr. '32s	1932* (Mgr)	DRAKE, Rodman L. '65	1964, 65 (Mgr)
CLARK, Russell I., Jr. '57	1956	DUNCAN, Angus M. '81	1979*, 80
CHASE, Porter B. '19	1919*	DUNLAP, John R. '14s	1912*
CLOVIS, David C. '56	1956	DUNN, G.B. '31s	1931*
CLOW, Harry B. '24	1924		
COGGER, Harold W., Jr. '57	1956, 57	### E	
COLE, Rufus M. '77	1976, 77		
COLES, Jonathan '68	1966, 67, 68	EARL, Edwin '29	1929* (Mgr)
COLLIER, Paul S., 3rd '71	1969, 70, 71	ECKERLE, Chris '02	1999, 00
COLLINS, Matt '03	2000*	EGAN, Robert B. '40	1938*
COMBS, Craig S. '71	1969, 70, 71	EMANUELSON, H.L., Jr. '51	1949*, 50*, 51
CONNELLY, John P. '82	1979*, 80, 81, 82	ENGEL, Richard L. '58	1958 (Mgr)
COYLE, Matthew N. '78	1976	ENGLAND, Daniel, Jr. '32	1930*, 31*, 32*
CREEKMORE, Edward F., Jr. '39	1939*	ESHELMAN, Herbert R., Jr. '36s	1933*, 34*, 35
CULLINAN, Craig F., Jr. '49	1949*		
CUMMINGS, Dexter '25	1923*, 24, 25*	### F	
CYRUS, Adam '02	1999, 00		
		FAYEN, George S., Jr. '53	1951, 52
### D		FEHR, Gerald F. '55	1953, 54
		FIFT, Henry H. '65	1964
DATOC, Patrick D. '85	1985	FISCHER, David D. '65	1964, 65
		FISHER, Robert C. '37	1935

FLINN, George H., Jr. '26s	1924, 25*, 26*	HANDREN, Frederick R. '61	1960
FOLEY, Charles T. '93	1992, 93	HARRIS, Joseph C. '44	1942* (2)
FORREST, Marshall W. '30	1928*, 29*, 30*	HARRIS, Richard '54	1954
FRANCO, James R. '89	1988*	HARRIS, Scott '88	1985
FULLER, R.H. '17	1917*	HARTFIEL, William F. Jr. '51	1950*, 51
FULTON, Alexander '04	2003, 04	HAVERSTICK, W. '34	1934* (Mgr)
		HAVILAND, Paul '27	1925*, 26*, 27*

G

		HAWKES, S. '??	1919*
GAINES, Francis S. '17	1915*, 16*	HEALEY, James T. '51	1949*, 50*, 51
GALLO, Ray E. '86	1984, 85, 86	HEINTZ, Robert E. '92	1989, 90, 91, 92
GAMBLE, David S., 3rd '32	1931*, 32*	HELTON, John C., Jr. '72	1970, 71, 72
GARDNER, Gibson '20	1920*, 21*	HEMKER, F. Roger '55	1953, 54
GARDNER, Robert A. '12	1911*, 12*	HERNANDEZ, Joe '08	2005, 06, 07, 08
GARDNER, Robert A., Jr. '43	1942*	HEWINS, Daniel F. '67	1966, 67
GARDNER, William H., 2nd '16	1914*, 15*, 16*	HILLENMEYER, Edward F. '90	1988*
GILISON, Alan N. '60	1958, 59, 60	HODGMAN, Charles L. '24	1924
GINAKAKIS, Tom '09	2006, 07, 08	HOGAN, Daniel B. '65	1963, 64, 65
GITCHELL, Joseph G. '92	1990*, 91, 92	HOLDING, James C. '55	1953
GOFF, James P. '86	1983, 84, 85, 86	HOLMES, Chris '07	2004, 05, 06
GOLDBERGER, Herman J. '35s	1933*, 34*	HOPONICK, Jeffrey J. '81	1979, 80, 81
GONZALES, Seve '10	2007, 08	HOUT, Thomas M. '64	1963, 64
GOODWIN, Jason '01	1998*	HOWARD, A.S. '31S	1930*
GOODYEAR, Robert M., Jr. '74	1972, 73, 74	HOWARD, Michael T. '72	1971, 72
GRAVELY, Edmund K. '42e	1940*, 41*, 42*	HOWSON, C.H., Jr. '30S	1930* (Mgr)
GRAVES, Robert B. '76	1973	HUDDLESTON, William H. '85	1982, 83, 84, 85
GRAY, R. '33	1933*	HUFFAKER, Stephen L. '97	1997
GRAY, Steve '05	2003, 04, 05	HULL, Gregory L. '92	1989, 90, 91, 92
GREER, Peter C. '62	1961	HUNDT, Nathaniel '07	2004, 05, 06, 07
GRISCOM, Clement A. '22	1920*	HUNTER, Robert E. '11s	1911*
		HUTTON, A.I. '49	1947*

H

I

HAKES, Taylor '09	2006, 07, 08		
HALL, Peter G. '00	1997*, 98*	INESON, Thomas P. '47e	1947*
HALLOWELL, J. Wallace, 3rd '51	1951 (Mgr)	ISRAEL, James C. '90	1988, 89, 90

J

JACOBS, Curtis D. '50	1947*
JAMISON, Paul B., Jr. '38	1935, 37*, 38*
JENNINGS, Frederick B. '14	1912*, 13*
JOHNSTON, George S. '48	1947*, 48*
JONES, Rees L. '63	1962 (Mgr)
JONES, Robert T., Jr. '61	1959, 60, 61
JOY, Homer '29S	1929*

K

KAMPF, Warren E. '89	1986, 87, 88
KEUTGEN, George O., Jr. '41s	1941*
KHAWAJA, Abdur R. '00	1997*, 98*, 99*, 00
KILPATRICK, William A. '44	1942* (Mgr)
KILREA, Walter C. '54	1952, 53
KIM, Brian '06	2003, 04
KNAPP, Alexander M. '29	1927*, 28*, 29*
KOHANSKY, Gregg E. '95	1993, 94, 95
KREMS, Daniel S. '98	1996, 97*, 98
KUNTZ, Robert W. '44s	1941*, 42*(2),42, 43*
KUNTZ, William R. '43s	1942* (2)

L

LANMAN, William K., Jr. '28s	1926*, 27*, 28*
LAPHAM, Nicholas '91	1990*
LARSEN, Clayton T. '80	1980
LARSON, Clayton T. '82	1979*
LAUCK, G.M., Jr. '38	1937*, 38*
LAWTON, Drew '81	1980
LEE, Howard B. '13S	1912*, 13*
LEE, Joseph A., Jr. '46m	1945, 46*
LEE, Kenneth E. '83	1980*, 81*, 82, 83
LEIBER, David P. '86	1983

LEIBOVIT, Jeffrey '77	1974, 75
LEVINSON, John O. '36	1934*, 35*, 36
LEVINSON, Jonathan B. '97	1994, 95, 96, 97
LEVY, Benjamin '04	2003, 04
LEVY, Daniel A. '06	2003, 04, 05, 06
LEWIS, Thomas M., 2nd '44	1942*
LINCOLN, John H. '68	1968 (Mgr)
LIPMAN, Arnold T. '54	1952, 53
LOBSTEIN, Henry P. '62	1960, 61, 62
LOMAS, Corey '07	2004, 05, 06, 07
LOMBARDO, Brian P. '81	1979*
LONG, Thomas F. '80	1977, 79, 80
LORD, William H. '48e	1945, 46*
LORENZE, Mark D. '88	1985, 86, 87, 88
LOVELL, Nathaniel T. '23	1921*
LOWE, Edward P. '83	1980*, 81*, 83
LUBAR, Charles G. '63	1961, 62, 63
LUNDELL, Ernest M. '55	1953, 54
LYSTADT, Scott E. '79	1977, 79

M

MacALLISTER, Ian B. '00	1997, 98, 99, 00
MARKWELL, Robert M. '18s	1917*
MARICK, Brandon R. '11	2008
MARTINSON, Ross T. '76	1975, 76
MARX, Ernest R. '72	1970, 71, 72
MATZA, Mark '07	2004, 05, 06, 07
McALEENAN, J. Austin '21s	1921*
McCARTHY, Thomas C. '11	2008
McCULLOUGH, Warrington B., 3rd '58	1956, 57, 58
McINERNEY, Brendan '37	1934*, 35*
McKEE, William S. '66	1966
McMILLAN, Howard I. '19s	1919*

MEISTER, Edward L. '40	1938*, 39*, 40*
MELOY, W.T. '28s	1928*
MEMMINGER, L., Jr. '44	1942*
MENNINGER, Charles N. '43	1941*
MERRIMAN, Buckingham P. '10	1911*
MERRITT, Haines R., Jr. '39	1937*, 38*, 39*
MERWIN, J. '31S	1930*, 31*
MEYER, Russell W., Jr. '54	1953
MEYERS, Bruce P. '67	1966, 67
MICHEL, Chris '03	2000*
MICKELSON, Nate '02	1999*, 00
MILES, John M. '88	1985, 86, 87
MONTERMOSO, Juan '95	1993, 94
MOORE, Colby '09	2006, 07, 08
MOORE, John J. '89	1986, 87
MORE, Timothy T. '67	1966
MOSSER, Karl E. '11	1911*
MOZELESKI, Frank S. '63	1962, 63
MUDGE, Dudley H. '17	1916*, 17*
MUIR, William K. '26s	1925*, 26* (Mgr)
MUNSON, Charles S., Jr. '37s	1934*, 35*, 37*
MYERS, Joseph M. '82	1979

N

NASSAU, Robert G. '81	1979*, 81
NEEDHAM, Christopher E. '90	1988, 89, 90, 91
NEITHAMER, Calvin D. '46	1946*
NIEGELSKY, Robert '76	1973, 74, 76
NILSON, George A. '63	1962, 63
NISSELSON, Peter M. '57	1956, 57
NORTON, J. Hughes, 3rd '69	1967, 68, 69 (Mgr)
NOYES, Frank '33	1933*
NOYES, Frank, Jr. '72	1970, 71, 72 (Mgr)
NOYES, Sidney W. '33	1931*, 32*, 33, 33*

O

ORDWAY, Richard '26	1925*
O'ROURKE, John F. '15s	1915*
ORSAK, Stuart '00	1997*, 98*
OXFORD, Larry B. '70	1968, 69, 70

P

PAGE, Chauncey O. '41s	1939*, 40*, 41*
PARKER, John E., Jr. '33	1931*, 32*
PARKER, Kennedy B. '36	1933*, 34*
PARKER, Lewis R. '28	1927*, 28*
PARSONS, James O., Jr. '40	1940*
PAYNE, Samuel G. '63	1961, 62, 63
PHILLIPS, Bruce J. '54	1952
PHILLIPS, James M. '60e	1958, 59, 60
PHILLIPS, S., Jr. '42	1941*
PIDGEON, Brian '83	1983
PIDGEON, Eugene J. '49	1948*, 49*
PIDGEON, Lawrence S. '85	1982, 85
PIERCE, Andrew '02	1999*
PIERCE, Brian P. '95	1993, 94, 95, 96
PIERCE, Richard deZ. '16	1914*, 15*, 16*
PINTO, Frank, Jr. '81	1980, 81
POLACKWICH, Robert J. '69	1967, 68, 69
POPOWITZ, Richard L. '94	1994
POTTER, Joseph '07	2004, 05, 06, 07

Q

QUINLAN, Robert F. '44	1942* (2)

R

RADER, Martin A., Jr. '67	1966 (Mgr)
RAGAINI, David M. '63	1961, 62, 63
RAMSEY, George K. '47	1945, 46*, 47*

RANDALL, Risher '50	1950*
RANKIN, H.P. '33	1933 (Mgr)
RASKA, William G., Jr. '81	1979*
REESE, J.D. '31	1930*, 31*
REGAN, Brian T. '00	1997*, 98, 99, 00
REIGELUTH, R.S. '39	1939*
REISSMAN, Rick '06	2003, 04, 05, 06
RESNIK, Burton B. '34	1933*, 34*
REWINSKI, Jon L. '81	1979, 80, 81
REYNOLDS, Jonathan W. '77	1975, 76, 77
RIZVI, Nader K. '97	1994, 95, 96, 97
ROBBINS, Todd B. '73	1971, 72, 73
ROBBINS, Walter S. '51	1949*, 50*, 51
ROBERTS, J.A. '29	1928*
ROBINSON, Joseph D. '57	1957 (Mgr)
ROBINSON, Thomas E. '57	1956 (Mgr)
RODEN, Lincoln, 3rd '52	1950*, 51, 52
RODGERS, Bertram J., 3rd '77	1976, 77
ROGERS, James G., 3rd '68	1965, 66, 67, 68
RUBIN, Brant '02	1999*, 00
RYAN, F.B. '28	1928*
RYDELL, John R., 2nd '67	1965, 66, 67
RYERSON, J.B. '??	1920*

S

SANDERSON, Chase O., Jr. '72	1970, 71, 72
SARGENT, Mark W. '75	1974, 75
SCHEMPP, Adam '03	2000*, 01, 02, 03
SCHUMACHER, Peter J. '00	1997, 98, 99, 00
SCOTT, J. Virgil, Jr. '41	1939*, 40*, 41*
SCOTT, Joseph C. '63	1963
SCOTT, Sidney '21	1919*, 20*, 21*
SEELEY, William P. '13	1913*
SEELYE, Theodore B. '73	1972, 73

SEIGLER, Morgan '99	1998, 99
SEMPLE, Harton S. '43	1942*
SEVERTSON, Mark A. '87	1984, 85, 86, 87
SHANLEY, Justin M. '89	1986, 87, 88, 89
SHAPIRO, Adam J. '94	1994
SHAW, Ed '03	2003
SHEEHAN, Colin D. '97	1994, 95, 96, 97*
SHERMAN, John A. '27	1927*
SHERRILL, Stephen C. '75	1975
SHIN, Jason '05	2003, 04, 05
SHURLEY, Burt R. '34	1933*, 34*
SIDEROWF, Andrew D. '87	1984, 85, 86, 87
SIEGLER, Joseph M. '99	1997
SIMON, Franklin '51	1951
SLADE, Grant H. '81	1979, 80, 81
SLATER, Thomas F. '66	1964, 66
SMALL, Robert J. '88	1985
SMITH,	1921* (Mgr)
SNYDER, Edward J. '66	1964, 65, 66
SPEERS, W. '31	1930*
SPENCER, S. Reid, 3rd '72	1970
STACKS, John S. '91	1991
STANLEY, George C. '13	1911*, 12*, 13*
STEINER, James P. '82	1979*, 80, 82
STEVENS, D.J. '54	1952, 53
STEWART, Charles K. '69	1969
STEWART, H.B. '28S	1928* (Mgr)
STEWART, William R. '65	1964, 65
STOCKHAUSEN, William E. '35	1934*, 35*
STRACKS, John S. '90	1988, 89, 90
STUCKY, William McD. '40	1940* (Mgr)
STURHAHN, Herbert C. '27s	1927* (Mgr)
SUISMAN, John R. '59	1957, 58, 59
SWEETSER, Jess W. '24s	1921*

SWOOPE, W.M. '31   1930*, 31*

T

TANGTIPHAIBOONTANA,
   Tommy '04   2003, 04

TERAVAINEN, Peter G. '78   1975, 76, 77

TETI, James '92   1992

THOMPSON, J. '??   1920*

THON, Richard M. '77   1974, 75, 76, 77

TIFT, Henry H., 4th '65   1964, 65

TOWNE, Frederic B. '35   1933*, 34*, 35*

TRANSUE, Oliver M. '34   1932*, 33, 33*, 34*

TRANSUE, Oliver M. '68   1968

TRIPLETT, Thomas McI. '62   1960

TUBBS, Chapin F. '12   1912*

TUTTLE, H. MacGregor Jr. '36s   1935* (Mgr)

TUTTLE, J.M. '2?   1925*

V

VARE, Edwin C. '56   1954, 56

VERITY, Calvin W., Jr. '39   1937*, 38*, 39*

VERNON, Murray, Jr. '54   1952, 53

VITT, Andrew '05   2003, 04, 05

VOLLERO, Robert A. '99   1997*, 98*

W

WALDO, C. Gilbert '12s   1911*, 12*

WALKER, John F. '61   1959, 60, 61

WARD, Seth C. '83   1980, 81, 82, 83

WARGO, Brad J. '94   1991, 92, 93, 94

WARNER, James A. '81   1979, 80, 81

WARNER, M. Pierpont '33   1931*, 32*, 33, 33*

WATKINS, Samuel '39   1939*

WATTLES, Frank E. '26   1924, 25*, 26*

WEATHERWAX, H. Law '34   1933, 33*, 34*

WEBBER, Thomas J. '83   1980*, 81*

WEISS, Theodore '60   1958, 59

WELLES, Edward O'M. '47   1945, 46*

WESCOE, Benjamin '10   2007, 08

WHEELER, Nathaniel '14   1913*, 14*

WHITE, Henry M., Jr. '50   1950*

WHITNEY, Ronald F. '68   1968

WILBOURNE, Douglas D. '85   1984

WILFORD, Robert S. '59   1957, 58

WILLIAMS, Arthur C. '43   1941*, 42*

WILLIAMS, Neel '04   2003

WILLNER, Henry S. '70   1968, 69, 70

WILLSTATTER, Richard '43s   1942* (2) (Mgr)

WILSON, Forbes K. '31s   1929*, 30*

WILSON, Holden '12   1912*

WILSON, J.

WILSON, Lyndon A. '36   1935*

WINTER, D.W. '21   1920*

WINTER, Edwin W. '21   1920*

WISE, Edmund N. '53   1953 (Mgr)

WISLAR, George R. '54   1952, 53

WOITESHEK, Edward '02   1999*

WOOD, William H., Jr. '43s   1942*

WRIGHT, F.H. '34   1932*

Y

YOSHIDA, Hirotoshi '85   1983

YULE, George G. '14s   1914*

— O —

Varsity Golf Letter Recipients, Women, 1981-2008

A

B

BARRAS, Charity '99 — 1996, 97, 98

BELL, Margret '98 — 1995, 96, 97, 98

BOLES, Cassie '11 — 2008

BRAKEMAN, Rachel '99 — 1996, 97, 98, 99

BROPHY, Ellie '08 — 2005, 06, 07, 08

BROWN, Kimberly '04 — 2001*, 02*

C

CARTER, Rebecca '94 — 1992, 93, 94

CASEY, S. Gillian '88 — 1986, 87, 88

CAVANAGH, Susan E. '84 — 1982, 83, 84

CAVENDISH, Sara J. '84 — 1983, 84

CHABNER, Elizabeth '89 — 1988*, 89

CHING, Janis S.L. '86 — 1984, 85

CONNERS, Clare '96 — 1994

COUGHLIN, Roxanne P. '82 — 1982

D

DAMGARD, Julie M. '93 — 1990*, 91, 92, 93

DAVIS, Jordanna '03 — 2000, 01, 02, 03

DEME, Della '04 — 2001*, 02*

DONOFRIO, Heather P. '91 — 1988, 89, 91

F

FARNUM, Elizabeth K. '85 — 1984

FISCHL, Wendy '86 — 1986

FISHER, Kate '98 — 1996, 97, 98, 99

FRANCUS, Andrea '82 — 1981, 82

G

GILL, Wendy P. '93 — 1990, 91, 92

H

HONG, Lindsay '08 — 2005, 06, 07, 08

I

IM, Erica '09 — 2006*, 07

J

JARVIS, Elizabeth S. '88 — 1985, 86, 87, 88

JEPSON, Anna '03 — 2002

JINKINS, Susan '86 — 1983, 84, 85

JOHN, Alice E. '84 — 1984

JOHNSON, Emily '00 — 1997, 98, 99, 00

JORDAN, Amy K. '88 — 1985

K

KENEFICK, Paula S. '90 — 1987

KENZIE, Michele L. '86 — 1985, 86

KISHBAUGH, Janet L. '84 — 1984

KLEIN, Regina B. '85 — 1984, 85

L

LANE, Mary K. '87 — 1986, 87

LEDOUX, Jayne M. '88 — 1985

LEE, Jeehae '06 — 2003, 06

LEE, J. Mi '94 — 1992, 93, 94

LEE, Taylor '10 — 2007, 08

LEVINE, Janet L. '88 — 1985 (Mgr)

M

MacKINNON, Vanessa '95	1994, 95
MAYA, Teresa '89	1986
MUNSON, Ellen '86	1983

O

OWERS-BRADLEY, Harriet, '11	2008
OZAWA, Yumi '87	1984, 85

P

PAPPAS, Lauren '08	2005*
PARK, Jean '03	2000*, 01*
PARK, Rosa H. '94	1992, 93, 94*
PATTERSON, Ashley J. '91	1988, 89, 90, 91
PAULIN, Ilona '98	1995, 96, 97, 98
PEARSALL, Melissa '91	1988*
PEPIN, Susan '87	1984 (Mgr)
PRINCE, Julie A. '94	1992
PRITCHARD, Ruthann '84	1984

R

REAVES, Katherine '05	2002
REILLY, Erin C. '85	1984
RESSLER, Lauren '06	2003, 04, 05, 06
RHODES, Marylee S. '81	1981
RINGUS, Daina '05	2002*
ROBERTS, Jennifer M. '87	1984, 85
ROLAND, Alyssa '11	2008
ROLLER, Anne '01	1998*, 99*
ROMERO, January '06	2003, 04, 05, 06
ROMPOTHONG, Chawwadee '00	1997, 98, 99, 00
ROSENBAUM, Mindy L. '85	1984, 85
RUSHER, Annie '94	1993, 94*

S

SCHOLZ, Annie '02	1999, 00
SCHRIEFER, Jenny '02	1999, 00, 01, 02
SEO, Sarah '02	1999, 00, 01, 02
SHAPIRO, Jessica '06	2003, 04, 05, 06*
SHIN, Cindy '07	2004, 05, 06, 07
SJOSTROM, Lisa A. '84	1984
SNOW, Meredith '96	1994
SPACKEY, Natasha '09	2006, 07, 08
SPOLYAR, Mary M. '89	1986, 87, 88, 89
STANLEY, Marion '07	2004, 05, 06*, 07*
STRAIN, Edwina '81	1981

T

TOTH, Cynthia A. '90	1987, 88, 89, 90

V

VOTAVA, Julie '95	1993, 94, 95

W

WALKER, Marylou '86	1985, 86
WEI, Stephanie '05	2002, 03, 04
WINSLOW, Andia '04	2002, 03*
WOHLFEIL, Tiffany '00	1997, 98*, 99*, 00*
WONG, Natalie '98	1995, 96, 97, 98

Y

YORK, Torrance B. '88	1985
YOUNG, Ashley '10	2007

Z

ZIMMER, Carmen '07	2004, 05*

— ◯ —

The Nineteenth Hole

Acknowledgments

This book has two authors, but it has truly been a collaboration of many individuals who have so generously shared with us their memories, materials, and expertise. At the heart of our project are the extended oral history interviews that we have been able to conduct with many of them. To date, the interviewees are Tom Beckett, Bill Beinecke, Gary Benerofe, Ed Brokner, Terry Calabrese, Carm Cozza, Heather Daly-Donofrio, Pete Dye, Gerry Fehr, Betsy Gentry, Paul Goldstein, Steve Gray, Bob Heintz, Rees Jones, R. T. (Bobby) Jones, Jr., Herb Kohler, Sam Kushlin, Bill Lee, Harry Meusel, "Mow" Moran, Mary Moan, Bill Neale, Bob Nagel, Phil Nelson, Herb Newman, Peter Oosterhuis, David Paterson, Peter Pulaski, Scott Ramsay, Ester Resnik, Jim Rogers, Roger Rulewich, John Schleicher, Dan Smith, Joe Sullivan, Jess Sweetser (by David Paterson), Bob Tettlebach, Ned Vare, Ken Venturi, and Al Wilson. All of these fascinating conversations are available online and in full at the Yale Golf History website. In addition, Jim Kreuttner, Ted Weiss, and Arthur "Ace" Williams provided us with written reminiscences that can be read at the website, and we have adapted portions of their stories into this book.

Our gratitude to the Department of Athletics must begin at the top with Athletics Director Tom Beckett, who recognized the value of such a project and sponsored us from the beginning. Forrest Temple, his Senior Associate Director, saw to it that we had funds for our research, and Geoff Zonder, the Athletics Department Archivist always quickly fulfilled our requests for checking facts and providing historical materials. Steven Conn, Assistant Athletic Director for Sports Publicity, has offered valuable advice and contacts.

At the golf course, David Paterson, Peter Pulaski, and Scott Ramsay have been unstinting in sharing their vast knowledge and their own materials about Yale golf.

Three undergraduates have given essential research assistance over several years. Jason Lindgren (Yale College, 2007) was our webmaster and stalwart associate from 2005 until his graduation in 2007. Jesse Bia (University of Rochester, 2009) supported us during the summer of 2007, and Adam Boles (Hamilton College, 2011) has been our able assistant in 2008 and 2009. Mary Smith, the Anthropology Department Administrator, has supported us throughout with her typical administrative competence and good cheer.

For contributions of original documents and photographs, we warmly thank Professor and Mrs. William Anderson, Ed Brash, Barbara Borsodi Gilbert, Betsy Gentry, Walter Kearns, Gerry Mullally, Bill Neale, Peter Rawson, Lincoln Roden, Jim Rogers, Frank Selva, Gareth Smith, and Ron Watts.

For contributions of photographs, we are grateful to Tom Greto, Peter Heald, Larry Lambrecht, and Scott Ramsay. We extend particular thanks to the Yale University Chief Photographer, Michael Marsland, who accompanied us on several circuits of the course to take photographs and who is beginning an extensive documentation of the course that we hope will result in a subsequent publication.

We owe a special debt of gratitude to George Bahto, author of one of the finest golf history books, *Evangelist of Golf: The Story of Charles Blair Macdonald* (Sleeping Bear Press, 2002). It is highly recommended for placing the Yale golf course construction in the context of Macdonald's life and design theories and his mentorship of Seth Raynor. For his book,

Bahto made original schematic drawings of all of the current Yale course holes as they may have appeared in 1926 when the course first opened. He has graciously allowed us to reproduce those drawings in this book.

Finally, just as prospects for publishing the book seemed most uncertain, we came upon an author's dream team. Heather Salome of MetaGlyfix is such a talented graphic designer that she could bring alive this story with her splendid layout. Kay Mansfield is an editor extraordinaire, and her keen eye and sharp red pencil have kept us on the grammatical straight and narrow. Jason Driscoll of Phoenix Press took an active interest in the project and shepherded it expeditiously and stylishly into production with his distinguished local family firm. They are partners all, and we feel fortunate to have benefitted from their talents.

About the watercolor illustrations and their artist

We are deeply appreciative to Callaway Arts and Entertainment for its permission to use several beautiful watercolor drawings by the gifted artist, Matthew Cook. He painted them after a visit to the Yale Golf Course in 1997. Cook is a graduate of the Kingston School of Art in England and is one of the most recognized illustrators of his generation. He has traveled the world with his sketchbook as expedition artist and has had a wide range of commissions from public agencies and private organizations. Cook has drawn stamps for The Royal Mail and sketches for *National Geographic*. He has been a staff illustrator for *The Times* (of London), which sent him to Iraq in 2002 and 2003 to follow British and American military units. His sketches and illustrations from that assignment have since been shown in several exhibitions.

The watercolors we have been given permission to use originally appeared in *Breaking 90 with Johnny Miller* (New York: Callaway Books, 2000). Matthew Cook's panoramic watercolor of the third and fourth fairways appears as the front and back cover of our book. The watercolor drawings within the book depict the following:

Page xiii — Warming up on the first tee and waiting for the starter's call.

Page 42 — Looking across the third and fourth holes' water hazard, which was created from the "great swamp" in Greist's nature preserve.

Page 62 — Sam Kushlin became a member of the Yale golf club in 1942 (at age thirty) at the end of Ben Thomson's tenure. In 2008 he was still playing, as seen in this image, although he says, "The best part of my game now is the shower."

Page 82 — A member of the grounds crew at work.

Page 136 — Golfer and cart crossing the bridge to the third fairway. In the late 1970s, carts were introduced by David Paterson, and the cart storage barn and cart paths were a gift of William S. Beinecke.

Page 170 — In 1983 Ben Crenshaw visited the course and was distressed to find grass growing in the bunker to the front left of the second (Cape) green, as well as in many other bunkers. The bunker restoration program begun by David Paterson and completed under Tom Beckett's Athletics Department directorship has remedied that problem.

Page 182 — Ringing the bell behind third green, which indicates that the green is all-clear. Looking back across the green, the rear of the clubhouse is visible. There is another all-clear bell behind the twelfth green.

Page 250 — John Godley on the fourth fairway.

About the Yale golf history website
http://webspace.yale.edu/Yale-golf-history

For more extensive documentation and updated materials about Yale golf history, we encourage readers to visit the archival website we have developed. There they will find more photographs, diagrams, written accounts, film clips, and published materials. Most important, the website has audio streaming of the oral history interviews we have conducted since 2004 with more than forty individuals who have been associated with Yale golf. Their stories and their views, in their own voices, are the most engaging and enduring testimony to Yale golf.

We are always updating, revising, and adding to the site, and we invite readers to contact us if they have materials and memories to share.

Replace divots.

Players must forbid caddies entering bunkers except when absolutely necessary, and at all times cover their own footprints.

Players must not climb sides of bunkers. Use the steps.

Out of bounds:
Over fence at the left of 13th green.
In parking space.

Press of
THE WILSON H. LEE COMPANY
Orange (New Haven), Connecticut

RAY TOMPKINS MEMORIAL
YALE GOLF CLUB
NEW HAVEN

Aug. 1, 1933
15000
93.00

◄——————— STYMIE GAUGE ———————►

RAY TOMPKINS MEMORIAL YALE GOLF CLUB

Self ....
Op'nt ....

HOLE	CHAMPIONSHIP COURSE	REGULAR COURSE	SHORT COURSE	PAR	STROKES	SELF	OP'T	SELF	OP'T
1	410	399	379	4	4				
2	365	349	338	4	14				
3	380	370	310	4	12				
4	440	426	309	4	2				
5	135	131	117	3	18				
6	440	332	308	4	8				
7	368	348	289	4	15				
8	415	409	372	4	6				
9	225	210	190	3	10				
	3178	2974	2612	34	OUT				
10	405	373	342	4	3				
11	375	320	320	4	13				
12	416	350	350	4	7				
13	190	190	190	3	16				
14	372	335	320	4	11				
15	188	170	135	3	17				
16	506	430	420	5	5				
17	425	382	382	4	9				
18	580	560	560	5	1				
	3457	3110	3019	36	IN				
	6635	6084	5631	70	TOTAL				

Date .... Attested ....

The first scorecard, 1926

About the first scorecard

The score card that appears in this book on the page facing is a reproduction of the first card for the present Yale Golf Course that opened in 1926. The card bears the title of the "Ray Tompkins Memorial Yale Golf Club." Our reproduction is from a 1933 printing, which, records show, cost the University $93.00 for 15,000 cards. The volume of the printing suggests the popularity of the course even in the early 1930s.

It is not clear why the "regular course" yardage and handicap stroke columns are in red, although this is presumably for ease of use. Noteworthy about the four brief regulations on its back cover is the near absence of marked out of bounds on the course — only the "parking space" and "over fence at the left of thirteenth green," referring to the boundary fence that still divides the Yale property from the New Haven Water Company land.

Most unusual to present-day golfers is the "stymie gauge," to use when the card was spread open to its full width of six inches. This was a common feature of scorecards of the era because the stymie was still part of the rules of golf in both Great Britain and the United States. In golf's early decades, balls were not marked on the putting green. As now, the player whose ball was further from the hole had to play first, and if he found his opponent's ball to lie in his putting line, he was forced to play around or over the ball. That is, either he could putt and hope that there was adequate break to curve his ball around his opponent's ball or he could use his niblick (something like today's wedges although less-lofted) to pitch his ball over the opponent's ball and run it up to the cup. Indeed, "laying a stymie" was a critical playing strategy. The photograph on page 4 is of a group of golfers gathered around an attempt to "play a stymie" at the New Haven Golf Course.

If the player made contact with his opponent's ball while trying to evade a stymie, he had to play his next shot from the point at which his ball came to rest. His opponent had the option of replacing his ball at the original spot or playing from where it came to rest. If a player put his opponent's ball in the hole, the opponent was considered to have holed out without an additional stroke.

The one exception was when a player's ball lay within six inches of an opponent's obstructing ball. Thus, scorecards were often cut to that length to serve as a stymie gauge, as we see with Yale's first card.

In 1938, the USGA experimented with a rule that any obstructing ball within six inches of the cup could be marked regardless of its distance to the other ball. However, it was not until 1952 that both the USGA and the Royal & Ancient Golf Club of St. Andrews, which is the rule-governing body in Great Britain, removed the stymie from their rule books.

About the authors

John A. Godley retired from four decades of medical practice in 1999. Since then he has played golf, painted, worked at Golf-Art.com, and enjoyed time with his wife, four children, and ten grandchildren. In preparing to write this book, he attended public schools in West Virginia and Ohio, college at Columbia University and medical school at Yale. He is a veteran of the US Air Force, where he did research in Aero-Space Medicine. In other words, until a short time ago, he had no idea that he was to be an author.

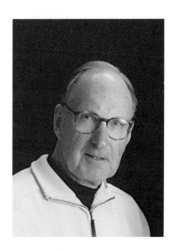

William W. Kelly is currently a professor of anthropology and the Sumitomo Professor of Japanese Studies at Yale. Neither has helped his handicap. His research and writing over the years have dealt with many topics of Japanese society and culture, most recently focusing on the role of sports in modern Japan. He began teaching at Yale in 1980, but it wasn't until the early 1990s, when an injury forced him to give up his passion for distance running, that he returned to one of his childhood sports, golf. He discovered the University course—and a new athletic passion.

Design, layout, and typography
by **H.G. Salome** of

Bristol, Vermont USA